# *Praise for*

# *Following His Lead*

*Following His Lead* is fantastic. It was one I couldn't put down. I felt like I really knew these people and wanted to be part of their group. Can't wait to see what God has in store for them in the next book.
—**Cindy Harrison**, Retired Missionary

\*\*\*

A very easy read and I would recommend it to each of my friends! I am an avid fan of Karen Kingsbury, and to be honest, since I've been following her over the last several years, I've not read any other authors. However, this was very much like hers, very fun, flowing, with Christ-centered content... very good! Now, I can't wait for your next book.
—**Diane Warren**, Pastor's Wife

\*\*\*

A true-to-life story of a young college graduate who decides to follow Jesus in every situation – both joyous and disappointing. Along the way, she discovers the security of God's faithfulness. Inspirational and delightful. Believable and interesting characters and deep relationships.
—**Carolyn Palmer**, Women's Small Group Leader

Join new college graduate, Cayden, as she learns to follow God's path for her. As we journey with Cayden, we, too, gain an understanding of God's ways and guidance. Baldwin has written an enjoyable read that challenges us to also be one *Following His Lead.*

—**Cynthia Heald**, Bible teacher and author of the *Becoming a Woman of… Bible studies.*

This book is everything it should be. It shows how different people can become the best of friends despite their culture or background. It also shows how God's goodness and His reasons He has for everything that happens in our lives. No matter the circumstances, He always brings people in our path to help give us extra encouragement and help point us in the right direction – His direction. And give us that extra encouragement we need. We are never alone when we have the Lord and He inserts other Christians in our lives to help us along and be a part of the blessings He provides. God always directs our paths. It may not be the way we want but we always end up back to Him. Also, no matter where anyone comes from or what their circumstance is, they can become a child of God by accepting Jesus in their heart. This definitely needs to be published. It has everything a good, Christian book should have and points everything and everyone to Jesus. I enjoyed every aspect of this book.

—**Jolene Campbell**, Preacher's Wife & Health Care Professional

# Following

# His

# Lead

Rhonda Baldwin

Published by KHARIS PUBLISHING, an imprint of
KHARIS MEDIA LLC.

Copyright © 2024 Rhonda Baldwin

ISBN-13: 978-1-63746-267-6

ISBN-10: 1-63746-267-0

Library of Congress Control Number: 2024946446

Scripture taken from the KING JAMES VERSION (KJV): King James Version, public domain.

All KHARIS PUBLISHING products are available at special quantity discounts for bulk purchase for sales promotions, premiums, fund-raising, and educational needs. For details, contact:

Kharis Media LLC
Tel: 1-630-909-3405
support@kharispublishing.com
www.kharispublishing.com

# Contents

Chapter 1................................................................11

Chapter 2 .............................................................15

Chapter 3 ............................................................. 20

Chapter 4 ............................................................. 26

Chapter 5 ............................................................. 28

Chapter 6 ............................................................. 32

Chapter 7 ............................................................. 36

Chapter 8 ............................................................. 42

Chapter 9 ............................................................. 48

Chapter 10 ........................................................... 52

Chapter 11 ........................................................... 57

Chapter 12 ........................................................... 63

Chapter 13 ........................................................... 66

Chapter 14 ........................................................... 74

Chapter 15 ........................................................... 82

Chapter 16 ...........................................................91

Chapter 17 ........................................................... 94

Chapter 18 ........................................................... 101

Chapter 19 ........................................................... 104

Chapter 20 ........................................................... 109

Chapter 21 ........................................................... 112

Chapter 22 ...................................................................116

Chapter 23 ...................................................................121

Chapter 24 .................................................................. 127

Chapter 25 .................................................................. 132

Chapter 26 .................................................................. 137

Chapter 27 .................................................................. 142

Chapter 28 .................................................................. 148

Chapter 29 .................................................................. 153

Chapter 30 .................................................................. 158

Chapter 31 .................................................................. 165

Chapter 32 .................................................................. 172

# Chapter 1

Cayden wondered for the millionth time why she had chosen to travel on such a busy holiday. She should have stayed with Marta and her family for one more night instead of tackling traffic on Memorial Day. But here she was sitting along I-95 north of Fredericksburg, Virginia with a car that had given up the ghost. Luckily, her parents had insisted on keeping her auto club membership up to date because one call and help was on the way. Even so, with this delay and the bumper-to-bumper traffic, she wouldn't get home until after dinner.

She and Marta had graduated from Liberty University in Lynchburg one week earlier. The last month had been packed with studying, finals, preparation for graduation, and boxing up all their accumulated stuff. But it was worth it because they were finally finished with school, homework, and APA formatting. After all the ceremonies and parties, they had loaded Cayden's Honda CR-V with their final personal belongings and headed north for about three hours to Winchester for some time with Marta's family. Thankfully, their parents had taken everything else when they'd returned home after graduation.

Marta had promised Cayden much deserved downtime and some mountain hikes, which appealed to Cayden before she tackled finding a job and settling down to "real" life. They had enjoyed a wonderful week of pampering by Marta's mom, Maria Vasquez, who was happy to have her girl home again. They slept late, ate well, and enjoyed just hanging out together. Four years earlier, they had been assigned as college roommates and now they were more like sisters than friends. Although they were opposites in a lot of ways, they were alike enough to appreciate each other. Whereas Cayden was

5'5" and slender, Marta was shorter with a rounder build. Marta's Hispanic heritage showed in her black hair and dark brown eyes, in contrast to Cayden's auburn hair and blue eyes. They both loved and served the Lord – one a Baptist and the other a Methodist. No matter the circumstance, they were always there for each other through the excitement and letdowns of college life along with the heartbreaks and triumphs of their personal lives. This past week had been a blessing for the girls to have one last time of togetherness before going their separate ways.

When the tow truck arrived, Cayden was ready to find out what was wrong with her car, get it fixed, and get back on the road. When she called her father, he was surprised the car was experiencing problems. It was only two years old and had been in fine running order when the mechanics inspected it one month earlier. But it wasn't fine now, and home was another two to three hours south depending on holiday traffic.

She had been born and raised in Virginia Beach. Her mom and dad, Meg and Paul Dewitt, had raised Cayden and her younger brother, Carter, in a home centered around God. Paul worked at Naval Air Station Oceana, and Meg was a part-time nurse at a local doctor's office. The family faithfully served God at Ocean Heights Baptist Church, where both children had come to know the Lord. Their modest ranch-style home in a quiet suburb was often the hub for Cayden and Carter and their friends to hang out. It was a home full of love and there were always goodies in the cookie jar. The Dewitt home was not only a mecca for kids but for pets as well. Over the years, they had adopted dogs, cats, goldfish, hamsters, birds, and even an iguana. The current pet residents were a German short-haired pointer named Skeeter and Sheba the cat.

At the repair shop, a skeleton crew was working the holiday shift and there was a long line of unhappy motorists waiting their turn. So, at eleven o'clock, with Chris Tomlin singing "Come Thou Fount" through her earbuds, Cayden settled in with her iPhone ready for a lengthy stay. Two hours later, realizing it had been a long time since breakfast at Marta's, she ventured next door for lunch at Taco Bell. She had just settled back in at the garage waiting room when the shop manager approached her with news about her car. Startled, she quickly removed the earbuds when he tapped her on the shoulder.

"Sorry to startle you, Ms. Dewitt. Must be some good music. You were so engrossed in it you didn't hear me call your name." The manager apologized with a tentative smile, realizing she obviously hadn't seen him approach.

"It is," Cayden agreed. "Do you know Laura Story? I was listening to my favorite song of hers, 'Blessings.' Guess my mind was somewhere else."

Smiling, he introduced himself. "I'm Don Mahoney, shop owner and manager. As a matter of fact, I do know Laura Story's music. We play it here in the shop along with other Christian artists." Sitting down in the chair next to Cayden, he continued, "I've got some not-so-bad but not-so-good news for you. Your CR-V needs a new serpentine belt, which isn't that big of a deal except with it being the holiday I can't get one until in the morning."

Cayden's expression must have shown how she felt inside because Mr. Mahoney immediately gave her shoulder a quick, reassuring pat. "There are several nice hotels and inns nearby. I know this wasn't what you were hoping for, especially on the first holiday of summer, but be glad it didn't happen in a less populated area. If you don't mind me suggesting, the Shamrock Inn is a nice, clean, affordable place with good food and the owner gives us a discount because she's a relative of sorts."

Unable to resist, Cayden asked how someone could be a *relative of sorts*. When Mr. Mahoney replied that the inn owner was a sister in Christ, Cayden felt a measure of calm she'd not felt since her car died. "Obviously, you know the Lord," she said with a bright smile. "I do too."

"Well, I guess that makes us relatives." He chuckled as his face broke into a smile." If you don't mind waiting, I'll ask my wife, who works here in the office, to take you to the inn and introduce you to Ellen Garver, the owner. I called and Ellen's holding a room for you just in case you want it, but no pressure. On holidays, a lot of the local hotels are booked solid, but Ellen had just gotten a cancellation."

Cayden realized she didn't have many options and truly appreciated the kindness this man was offering her. "If your wife doesn't mind taking me to the inn, that would be great. You all have been so kind, and I really appreciate it."

"It will be about thirty minutes before Beth, my wife, is ready to go. You might want to let your parents know what's happening. If I had a daughter in this position, I would be anxious to know how things were going." He gave her another quick smile as he headed back out into the garage.

Cayden wandered over to look out the window, sighing heavily over this unexpected turn of events. When she thought about the song she'd been listening to, she suddenly realized how many blessings were hers in this whole situation. She could have broken down in the middle of nowhere with no cell signal. She could have been stranded in the middle lane of I-95 with no way to get off the road. She could have lost control of the car when the belt broke and wrecked, injuring herself and others. Instead, God's hand was evident in where the car had broken down and her ability to maneuver off the road to safety. He had led her to this establishment operated by a fellow Christian, who was kind and caring. With these thoughts swirling in her head and heart, she called her dad and explained the situation. He was surprised to hear her so upbeat until she explained how God was guiding her in each step of the way. After assuring him that she would call as soon as she was settled at the inn, she ended the call and glanced at a nearby bulletin board. Smack dab in the center of the board was an advertisement for a church secretary.

During the last months of school, Cayden had spent a lot of time thinking and praying about what was next in her life. She was excited to find a job and hoped to find an apartment as soon as she started receiving paychecks. While many of her classmates had ambitions to find big jobs and make lots of money, she truly wanted to find a way to serve God with her talents and education. Though she didn't feel God was calling her into a particular ministry or to the mission field, she knew He was calling her to some type of service. Her office skills were more than sufficient and her ability to organize was off the charts. But most importantly, her heart was dedicated to doing God's will and finding the path He had for her.

When she saw the advertisement, her heart beat faster. Could a church secretary position be the answer – could *this* church secretary position be the answer? First, she would have to learn more about the church and its beliefs and reputation in the community. There was no telling how long the ad had been on the board. Maybe Mrs. Mahoney would know. Wouldn't that be something if this road trip detour led to her first job?

# Chapter 2

*A*t two o'clock on the dot, Beth Mahoney came around the corner into the waiting room and zeroed in on Cayden. "Hi, I'm Beth. And you must be Cayden. I'm sure you're more than ready to go. We strive to make this waiting room as friendly as possible, but it's still just that – a place for people to wait when all they want to do is get back on the road. Let's scoot on over to the Inn. Knowing Ellen, she'll have tea and scones waiting and that's something you don't want to miss. The guys put your luggage in my car, which means we're all set to fly."

Cayden was surprised at the small woman standing before her. Mrs. Mahoney hadn't taken a breath from "Hi" to "fly." Compared to Mrs. Mahoney, Mr. Mahoney was a very quiet, calm man. Maybe it *was* true that opposites attract. At any rate, Cayden knew immediately that she liked this petite, powerful woman and her energy.

"Thank you so much for making time to take me over to the inn. I hope you don't mind that your husband volunteered your services." Cayden wanted to make sure Mrs. Mahoney knew how much her willingness to help was appreciated.

"First, you must call us Beth and Don. Even though we're old enough to be your parents, we're plenty young at heart," Beth replied with a wink. "I love the excuse to leave work early and to get to know another of my sisters in Christ. Also, getting to spend some time with Ellen and enjoy some of her baked goods is a plus. So, not to worry – I'm happy we're able to help. I believe God puts us in the right place at the right time to help others, and this is one of those times. Makes my heart sing!"

Again, Cayden was surprised at the exuberance of this woman she'd only just met; but she was enjoying Beth's company. In fact, she had to admit that her spirit was uplifted just interacting with Beth. She wasn't surprised when Beth led her to a bright orange MINI Cooper that fit her personality to a tee – small, fiery, and ready to go.

In less than fifteen minutes, they arrived at an older two-story cottage with yellow siding, black shutters, and the most amazing flowerbeds. The riot of spring flowers added just the right touch of color to complement the lovely inn. The sense of welcome that began upon driving up in front of the inn continued upon entering the foyer where they were met with the most wonderful fragrances. Cayden was sure she had never smelled anything as alluring in her life as she followed Beth down the hall to a small breakfast nook next to the kitchen. The table was set for afternoon tea with scones, breads, jam, curds, and other delectables along with individual pots of hot tea. Their hostess and innkeeper, Ellen Garver, stepped into the room from outside followed by a small black and white dog. Upon seeing her guests had arrived, she hurried forward with a gentle smile and eyes full of merriment.

In a gentle Irish brogue, Ellen greeted them, "Oh my, you snuck up on me. Usually, Molly lets me know when we have guests, but she was too busy running around the backyard to pay proper attention." After giving Beth a hug, she turned to Cayden and introduced herself and her small dog. "I'm Ellen Garver, this is Molly, and you must be Cayden. Welcome to the Shamrock Inn."

Cayden shook Ellen's hand and couldn't stop herself from giving Molly a friendly pet, which was met with a satisfied sigh. "I'm happy to meet you and really appreciate your saving a room for me. Your inn is lovely and so inviting, and whatever you've been baking smells heavenly."

Ellen smiled and turned toward the front of the house. "Why, thank you. You'll be eating some of those goodies in just a minute, but first things first. Let's get you to your room so you can have a minute or two to regroup. You've had a rather eventful day – perhaps even a 'memorial' day." She couldn't help chuckling at her small play on words, but Cayden found herself agreeing wholeheartedly. It had been quite a day, and the day was still young.

The room to which Ellen led Cayden and Beth was in the back of the house. If Cayden thought the flowers out front were amazing, she had no words to describe the profusion of colors that met her when she looked out the windows. The landscaping was tastefully done so that the yard was a welcoming extension of the house. Guests were drawn outside to enjoy the flowers, sit on a bench or a swing to relax, read a book, or enjoy conversation. Her room was large with a small sitting area and a private bath. It was clean, comfortable, lovely, inviting, and just what Cayden needed to wind down and organize her thoughts.

"This is perfect and very much appreciated," she said while continuing to take it all in. "I have a feeling all of the hotels would have been booked solid for the holiday."

Giving Cayden a quick side hug, Ellen replied, "Well, Molly and I are certainly glad you're here. Why don't you get settled in, freshen up, and meet us back downstairs in say fifteen minutes?"

"That sounds wonderful," Cayden quietly agreed. "I can't wait to taste whatever it is I've been smelling since we came through the front door!" As Ellen and Beth headed out the door, Molly lingered until Ellen called her name. It seemed Cayden had made yet another friend in Fredericksburg.

She joined Beth and Ellen in the breakfast nook where the other two ladies had been catching up on what had been happening in their lives lately. Even though they attended the same church, it wasn't always possible to touch base as regularly as they would have liked. This was particularly true of Beth and Ellen since Beth was a Sunday school teacher for the primary age children and sang in the choir while Ellen worked in the nursery and was currently leader of the ladies' fellowship group.

Their conversation jogged Cayden's memory about the ad she'd seen on the bulletin board in the repair shop. She had planned to ask Beth about it but had gotten sidetracked on the drive over to the inn. After pouring herself a cup of tea and adding a scone with clotted butter to her plate, she decided now was the perfect time to ask. "I was wondering if you knew anything about Southside Baptist Church here in Fredericksburg."

When the ladies started laughing, Cayden wondered if she'd missed a private joke until Beth told her that they both attended Southside. "In fact, we were just talking about some upcoming events and special services. Why do you ask? Do you know someone who attends Southside, that is besides your two new best friends here?" Grinning at Cayden, she waved her arm to include herself and Ellen.

"Really? You're both members of Southside Baptist? Earlier at the garage I saw an advertisement on the bulletin board for a secretary at your church. I guess it makes sense that the ad would be on a church member's board," Cayden replied.

Giving Cayden a hopeful look, Beth asked, "Are you in the market for a secretarial job? Our current secretary, Gail Marchand, is ready to retire. She and her husband have bought a house at Nags Head and are anxious to move. They're moving closer to their daughter and her family. Pastor Harwell made the announcement yesterday morning and asked us to share the information. We just put the ad on the board this morning."

"Just to be clear, are you saying that you might be interested in this particular position," Ellen asked with a similar look on her face as Beth had.

Taking another bite of her scone and a sip of tea, Cayden took her time answering. "Well, I could be. I need to know more about the church and what it teaches, but I'm thinking you ladies can fill me in on that." There ensued a brief history of Southside Baptist Church and its pastor, Greg Harwell. By the time the scones were eaten, and their tea was growing cold, Cayden knew the church believed in solid biblical doctrine and the pastor led his flock with graciousness and love.

As Beth rose to help Ellen clear the table, she asked, "Would you want to meet with Pastor Harwell? I could call and see if he's available for a chat tomorrow morning." She joined Ellen in the kitchen to give Cayden a few minutes to think. This was sort of a big deal for a young person looking for her first job.

When she and Ellen returned to the table, Cayden asked them if they would pray with her that God would show her what He would have her do. Meeting with the pastor wouldn't be a commitment on either side but it was a big step for her.

Ellen reached out her hands to Cayden and Beth, bowed her head, and began to pray on Cayden's behalf. It was always best to go to the Father before taking the next step. When Ellen said "amen," Cayden looked at the two ladies with shining eyes and a big smile. "If your pastor could meet with me tomorrow, I would be happy to talk with him," she said with joy in her voice.

Beth made the call and returned five minutes later with an appointment for Cayden to meet with Pastor Harwell at nine o'clock the next morning. Ellen volunteered to take Cayden to the church and after her interview to take her to the repair shop to pick up her car. And just like that a plan was in place for her first real job interview.

It was after five o'clock by the time Beth left the inn. Cayden made her apologies to Ellen and returned to her room to spend some time alone with God and call her parents to fill them in on everything that had transpired in the course of this one amazing day. As she was turning to the book of Psalms, the day played out like a movie. Or maybe it was more like a puzzle solving itself. It started out with what seemed a terrible inconvenience, but it was amazing to see God's hand throughout each step. Where her car broke down, which shop the car had been towed to, the holiday delay for obtaining the needed part, someone cancelling a reservation at the inn, and the shop owner called at just the time to reserve it for her. She had met three wonderful Christians and one little dog that already felt like friends. The church secretary job was posted the same morning in the shop where she landed, she had seen the ad, and now she was going to meet the pastor to discuss the job.

The words to Laura Story's song "Blessings" came to her, and she knew beyond a shadow of doubt that they were true. Trials, such as a car breaking down on a busy interstate, could be God's mercy in disguise. Even if the job didn't pan out, this was one day Cayden would never forget because she had seen God's hand moving in her life and it was awesome.

# Chapter 3

*T*uesday morning found Cayden excited to see what the day held for her. After telling her parents how everything had happened the day before and letting them know she was meeting with Pastor Harwell, they were just as excited. There was nothing more important to them than to know their children were following God's will. And Fredericksburg was just a little over two hours away, which meant an easy day trip to visit their only daughter if she wound up locating there. They had prayed with her and made her promise to call as soon as her meeting was over.

When she went downstairs, it was still early but Ellen was busy in the kitchen getting breakfast ready for her guests. She had told Cayden that she believed God had blessed her with the inn so that she could minister to others, which she did with her pleasant personality, and her ability to put people at ease, not to mention her marvelous baking. Ellen greeted Cayden with a big smile and told her to help herself to the pastries already set out on the table. Cayden grabbed a cinnamon roll and coffee before heading to the backyard and a bench she'd been eying since arriving yesterday afternoon. With her Bible and breakfast, she settled in for some quiet time with her Lord. Before she knew it, Ellen was reminding her they would need to leave in twenty minutes. Thanks to her quiet time, Cayden was refreshed and joyful as she prepared to meet Pastor Harwell.

After one last pat on Molly's head, Cayden followed Ellen to her red Volkswagen Beetle. She realized again what a surprising woman her hostess was and thanked God for putting Ellen in her life. Both ladies were quiet as they drove the short distance from downtown Fredericksburg to the Three-mile Fork area. Ellen must have sensed Cayden's need to mentally and spiritually prepare for meeting Pastor Harwell, which gave her an opportunity to pray silently as she drove through town.

Cayden's Google search the night before had taken her to Southside Baptist's website where she read about the history of the church and Pastor Harwell's background. Everything she'd seen made her even more comfortable with the possibility of not only pursuing to work there but to be a member of the congregation. Their doctrine was sound, and it appeared the congregation was involved in several community outreaches that piqued her interest. They had a thriving youth group and a young adult ministry. Just the thing to get her acclimated to a new home, new church, and a new job.

Within minutes, Ellen was pulling into a parking spot in front of the church. Cayden asked her if she would mind praying one last time for God's guidance in all that would take place that day. After a brief prayer and a small hug, they walked into the church armed with the knowledge God was in control and his best was all they wanted.

Pastor Harwell met them in the lobby with a smile and handshake. Ellen introduced him to Cayden before excusing herself as she headed to the nursery to straighten up from Sunday's services.

After ushering Cayden into his office and offering her coffee, Pastor Harwell said, "I heard from Beth that you had a very interesting Memorial Day. The interstate around here is terrible on most days but it's something to avoid on a holiday. You were blessed to wind up at Don Mahoney's repair shop. That man is a crackerjack mechanic but more importantly he's a true Christian gentleman."

Cayden was shaking her head in agreement. God had clearly shown her how things could have worked out, which made her even more thankful for how they had ended up. "Don treated me like his daughter even before he knew I was his sister in Christ. He, Beth, and Ellen have gone above and beyond anything I could have expected from strangers, and I'm truly thankful for their intervention on my behalf. It was almost worth my car breaking down just to stay at Ellen's inn. Have you ever tasted her scones?" Realizing she was babbling, which was something that sometimes happened when she was nervous, she smiled and stopped talking.

"As a matter of fact, my wife and I make it a point to stay at the Shamrock Inn a couple of times each year. We tell Ellen we need a little get away time, but we're really there for her scones, muffins, and her wonderful breakfasts. But don't tell her. We'll let that be our little secret." It was as if he recognized she was nervous and was giving her time to feel comfortable, and it worked. She was visibly more relaxed as she laughed, agreeing to keep his secret.

"Beth mentioned you were heading home from Winchester, but she didn't fill in any other details. I'd love to hear how you wound up in Fredericksburg and now here in my office." As Cayden explained her detour to Winchester before going home from college and all that had transpired since, Pastor Harwell just smiled and shook his head. "Do you ever wonder if God has a sense of humor? Or if he doesn't just love to see his children amazed by his love? I mean you can clearly see his hand through each step of your journey."

Laughing, Cayden agreed. "He loves to give us what's best for us, just like my dad does. But when dad can throw in some sweet surprises along the way, he enjoys seeing my reaction. So, I guess our Heavenly Father does the same thing and enjoys our pleasure when we finally see what He's doing. What an awesome thought!"

The mention of her dad reminded her of their earlier conversation. "Oh, I almost forgot. My dad spoke with our pastor about all that happened yesterday and my meeting with you today. Pastor said to tell you hello." Her eyes twinkled as she saw the look of surprise cross his face.

Taken aback, Pastor Harwell asked, "Who's your pastor?"

"Rayfield Vincetti." Cayden couldn't help but laugh out loud at his expression.

"Ray? Wow! That's a blast from the past. How's he doing? I don't think I've seen Ray since we ran into each other about twenty years ago at a retirement party for one of our professors. We were roommates at Pensacola Christian College for our junior and senior years." Smiling, he threw up his hands with a sigh of resignation. "I know how much Ray loves to joke and can only imagine the stories he had to tell. That preacher can't pass up the chance to share a good story."

"You know him well! But there wasn't anything too embarrassing." Enjoying the ease of their conversation, she realized those stories had helped to make her more comfortable with Pastor Harwell. He had been a typical college student, and that she could relate to. "Pastor Ray had a health scare a few years ago but he's healthy and as lively as ever. And, just to put your mind at ease, after telling a few stories, he had nothing but praise for you and your dedication to the Lord."

"You know, Cayden, I can tell just from listening to you that you love the Lord. Want to tell me about the day you accepted him as Savior and a little about your Christian service?" Pastor Harwell asked as he settled back in his chair to hear her story.

Cayden hesitated for only a second before she explained how at age eight, she had asked Jesus into her heart. It was Christmas night, and she had asked her mom why they celebrated Jesus' birthday. After her mother explained that Jesus, God's son, had died so that her sins could be forgiven, she had prayed asking him to forgive her and to come into her heart. She was baptized two weeks later. Over the years, she had assisted in junior church, sung in the choir, been a counsellor a Christian summer camp, and served as president of her high school Bible Club. But her favorite ministry was working alongside her parents with the senior citizens at her home church.

After a few moments of general conversation, Pastor Harwell filled Cayden in on what the church secretary's job entailed. It wasn't just typing and filing. The secretary assisted in any area where there was a need including helping with the budget, creating presentations, setting up dinners, arranging functions, and assisting the staff. There was only one other paid member of the church staff, Youth Pastor Daniel Garrett. Pastor Harwell indicated that Daniel didn't require much assistance but would ask when he did.

As they talked, Cayden's excitement grew. The pay was more than she'd expected, and the work sounded perfect for her skillset. Most of all, everything they'd discussed painted a picture of a place where she could serve the Lord and make a difference. She hesitated to ask but couldn't help herself. "Beth mentioned that you let everyone know your secretary was retiring during Sunday services. Do you have an idea how long you will wait until you decide who to hire? I'm not trying to push you into a decision, but my plan is to hit the ground running when I get home looking for a job."

"Have you prayed about this? Not just the job but about relocating to a strange place and into a position that might not fully utilize your education. That's a lot and it deserves proper consideration and prayer." Pastor Harwell gazed at her with questions in his eyes.

"Yes sir, I've prayed. My family's been praying, and Beth and Ellen have been praying too. In fact, by now, I feel sure everyone on the prayer chain at my church back home is praying." A warm feeling spread through her as she thought just how much support she had.

After a moment of quiet contemplation, Pastor Harwell said, "There was one thing I didn't tell everyone on Sunday. Gail is anxious to train her replacement quickly so that she and her husband are free to assist her daughter, Monica, who has been diagnosed with diabetes. They have sold their house and are moving to Nags Head, where Monica lives, to assist with their grandchildren and anything else Monica needs. Gail told me Sunday night she was praying God would send her replacement pronto. So, I met with the deacons and trustees yesterday morning to fill them in and make sure they would be good with a quick turnaround. They gave me authority to hire with only me interviewing. That might not sound big but it's unusual for a pastor to have that much leeway in hiring. Gail, the deacons, trustees, and I started praying immediately. In fact, I'd say it was right about the time your serpentine belt broke yesterday morning that we were in earnest prayer for a new church secretary. I've prayed, you've prayed. Do you believe this is where God has for you to serve?"

Cayden began to cry and laugh at the same time before answering. "Yes sir. Yesterday, when I saw the ad on the board, everything in me started rejoicing but I didn't understand why. Then, step by step, God showed me how He has been guiding me to have me here today."

"Well, young lady, there's only one question left. When can you start?" When she only stared at him, he continued with a grin. "Would next Monday be too soon? Gail will be back in the office tomorrow and she'll get things ready to start your training."

"Monday would be great. I'll get home today and start making arrangements. I'm so excited! Please know how much I appreciate this opportunity," she said as Ellen came back in the office. Cayden grabbed her in a bear hug and shared the good news – she had the job.

Ellen didn't look at all surprised. "When Beth and I started seeing the path God had you on yesterday, we both felt it was leading to this. I could tell from Beth's expression that she realized it about the same time I did."

"So, that was why you both looked so odd during tea yesterday. I wondered but didn't know you well enough to ask," Cayden replied with a big smile. "Now I need to find a place to live. Know of any cheap apartments?"

"As a matter of fact, I do. Beth called me last night and we were both convinced this was where God was leading. She said to tell you they have a one-bedroom apartment over their detached garage they hope you'll consider renting. Beth is at the shop just waiting to hear everything and talk you into renting the apartment." Ellen was fairly beaming as she shared this bit of news.

"Just another piece of the puzzle falling into place!" Pastor exclaimed. He was never surprised at God's goodness, but he sure loved seeing it work out right before his eyes.

# Chapter 4

On the way to the repair shop, Ellen and Cayden couldn't stop chattering back and forth, exclaiming over how God was so clearly leading Cayden just as she'd asked Him to do. Upon arriving, they were joined by Beth and the chattering continued until Don came in the office to see what all the commotion was about. While he didn't chatter with them, he certainly did seem satisfied with what he saw unfolding before him.

"Have you told her about the apartment yet?" He and Beth had discussed it last night and again this morning and were hoping Cayden would take them up on their offer of the apartment. They had included the apartment over their detached two-bay garage so that Beth's niece could use it while attending the University of Mary Washington. She had graduated a year earlier, and the apartment remained vacant. The rent would be minimal, and he would like to be able to help Cayden if possible.

Beth gave him a playful shove before letting him know that Ellen had filled Cayden in on the details. Not to be deterred, Don continued. "So, would you like to take a look? The rent will be next to nothing, and we would enjoy having you nearby. Tell you what. It's eleven o'clock and you gals are probably getting hungry. Why don't you call in an order for Lucia's to deliver pizza at the house – my treat? That way, you can tour the apartment and discuss the particulars over lunch." Don knew Lucia's pizza would seal the deal with Beth and Ellen and he counted on a recently graduated college student to go for it with no problem. "And when you get back, Cayden's vehicle will be ready to go."

They piled into Ellen's Volkswagen, with Cayden in the backseat, and talked all the way to Beth's. Located in the Ferry Farms area of Fredericksburg, the large split-foyer house sat on three acres with a detached two-car garage set to the right and back of the house. The house was beautiful and relatively new. A stone walkway led from the cement driveway to the detached garage and the stairway that led to the upstairs apartment. Cayden fell in love as soon as Beth opened the apartment door. The living room was spacious with big windows allowing sunshine to stream in. Directly off the living room was a nice size kitchen with stainless steel appliances including a dishwasher. The bedroom was plenty big enough for her furniture, and the bathroom had lots of counter space. There was even a stackable washer/dryer unit off the kitchen area.

Over pizza, Beth explained the terms for leasing the apartment, which were more than reasonable. Cayden asked when she could sign the lease and get the keys. Business out of the way, three happy ladies enjoyed lunch and their new friendship. Cayden had found a home.

Don was true to his word and had Cayden's car ready when they returned to the shop. She paid what seemed like a very small repair bill and promised to text them when she arrived safely home. After giving hugs all the way around, she got in her car and headed toward I-95 south and home. That's when it hit her that the next time she was in Fredericksburg it would be *home*. Wonder of wonders!

# Chapter 5

efore Cayden knew it, she was pulling into her parents' driveway. With her mind so full of everything that had happened and everything to be done, the trip didn't seem to take long at all. To-do lists were floating around in her head as she opened the door and walked straight into her mom's arms. Happy tears mingled with excited bits of conversation as the two women hugged and laughed.

"Meg, let the girl breathe," she heard her dad's booming voice proclaim, "and let me give her a hug." She was passed to her dad and more tears flowed. It wasn't until her brother, Carter, entered the kitchen asking when they were going to eat that everyone calmed down enough to get their bearings and carry on a reasonable conversation.

When all of Cayden's things were stowed away in the room she'd grown up in, she took a break to get her bearings. Just a few days ago, she was a little anxious wondering what the summer would hold. And now, here she was getting ready to move to a new town and start a new job at a new church and, hopefully, meet lots of new friends. God had once again amazed her at how He continued to lead and direct, even amongst all her anxiety and fretting. She closed her eyes and prayed, thanking Him for loving her and caring about her future. What was that verse in Jeremiah? They'd discussed it in chapel just prior to graduation. She grabbed her phone to search for the verse and look it up in the Bible that was always on her nightstand. There it was – Jeremiah 29:11, "For I know the thoughts that I think toward you, saith the Lord, thoughts of peace, and not of evil, to give you an expected end." Even after seeing it over and over in her life, it never failed to astound her that God cared about her and had plans for her. It appeared those plans would begin in earnest on Monday, and she was ready for this new adventure.

The next day Cayden invited Carter to lunch at the restaurant of his choosing. Even though Chic-fil-A was his hands down favorite place to eat, working there most days after school satisfied his craving for chicken, so he opted for pizza at a shop not far from their house. This would also maybe leave some time for a quick tennis match, something he'd missed while his sister was away at college. Carter enjoyed Cayden's company and absolutely loved teasing her or pulling pranks on her. After all, why did a guy have an older sister unless it was to pester her? Because, let's face it, he knew how much she adored him and that she would take anything he dished out with grace. That didn't mean she wouldn't retaliate at some point in the future, which made it even more fun.

Two hours later, the brother/sister duo returned home happy with their time together. While Carter had looked forward to Cayden living back home, maybe it wouldn't be too bad with her only two hours away in Fredericksburg. Day trips to visit Cayden with his girlfriend, Clarissa, would be a must. After all, he would be graduating in a couple of years and then heading to college or maybe enlisting in the Marine Corps. Life as the Dewitt family had known it would be drastically reshaping. He found himself wishing he felt confident in God's leading like his sister did.

The rest of the week flew by, and Saturday morning dawned bright and sunny – the perfect day for a road trip. Everything was packed in her car and her dad's truck. After a quick breakfast and a special prayer for safe travel and joyous new beginnings, Cayden and her family headed north to Fredericksburg.

Cayden's mom rode with her, so they had some time to visit and come up with a plan for getting her apartment set up. Since the apartment came furnished with living room furniture and a dinette set, the main things to buy would be linens and items for her kitchen. Of course, there would be the trip to the grocery store to stock up on essentials. Hopefully, by dinnertime, she would be settled in her new home.

Her new friends outdid themselves to make Cayden welcome and to make her parents at ease about her new situation. Beth and Don had invited them, along with Ellen, for a cookout that evening so they could fellowship and get to know one another. Ellen had insisted Cayden's parents and Carter stay at the inn as her guests, which would give Cayden some time to settle in, recharge, and prepare for church on Sunday. Everyone hit it off immediately and good food laced with easy conversation rounded out the day. By the time darkness began to fall, they were all ready to call it a day, and Cayden retired to her new bedroom relishing how much had come together so quickly. She grabbed a quick shower before climbing into bed. Weariness quickly overcame her, and she fell asleep praying. Tomorrow was going to be an exciting day!

Southside Baptist was a lovely church with a campus consisting of the church and an annex housing classrooms, a large fellowship hall, and a gymnasium. Upon arriving Sunday morning, they were greeted by Pastor Harwell and his wife, Marietta. After a quick tour of the facilities, they were ready to join their Sunday school classes, which would begin in ten minutes. Cayden was looking forward to meeting the church staff and the people who would comprise her church family. As would be expected, she did have a few butterflies, which were quickly quieted when she entered her classroom and was embraced by two young ladies Marietta had asked to help her settle in. They made quick work of introducing Cayden to everyone before their teacher, Jeff Carson, quieted the group and opened in prayer.

Her own personal welcoming committee consisted of Ila Bennett and Allison Lambert. Ila was about the same height as Cayden but with a bit more padding in all the right places. She loved the Lord and reveled in the life God had given her. At home in her own skin, Ila never met a stranger and was quick to jump on the "glass half full" wagon. Otherwise, her job as a registered nurse at the Veterans Health Administration might have been hard to handle at times. That attitude also gave her the insight and compassion to assist patients and their families with a positive attitude and a helping spirit.

Allison Lambert, known as Allie to her friends and family, was pretty much the opposite of Ila. Slender and taller than Ila by a few inches, she had long strawberry blonde hair and green eyes. Opposites attract came to mind when seeing the two young women together. Allie was also poised and confident but quieter and with a less forceful nature. Where Ila loved being on the front line to not miss a thing, Allie preferred to stand in the background and quietly observe. Two years into her elementary school teaching career, Allie found this particular trait helpful when working with third graders.

Both Sunday school and the worship service passed in a bit of a blur until Cayden realized she wasn't really taking it all in. This was her new church home and her new church family. But more importantly, this was where she would be worshipping God and serving Him in whatever capacity He led her to fill. She breathed a quick but fervent prayer for His hand to continue guiding her and for faith to follow His lead. At the end of the service, Pastor Harwell invited her and her family to come forward so everyone could meet them and to offer a special prayer for Cayden as she started this new ministry as church secretary.

After a quick steakhouse dinner and lots of parting hugs, Cayden waved goodbye one last time as her dad's truck disappeared around the corner. What an emotional day this had been, and it was only two o'clock. Since evening service wasn't until six, she quickly made sure her outfit for work tomorrow was ready, set an alarm to wake her in plenty of time to get dressed for church, laid down on her couch, and fell sound asleep. She wanted to be well rested for her first day of work.

# Chapter 6

*G*ail Marchand had not been at church Sunday because she and her husband, Anthony, were at their daughter's home for the weekend. Cayden entered the office Monday morning expecting to meet someone who looked a lot like her Grandma Dewitt, but Gail was nothing like Grandma. She was a little over 5' tall with lovely red hair cut in a short pixie style and her eyes were cornflower blue. With a quick smile and hug, Gail welcomed Cayden and set about making her comfortable before jumping into her first training session. Cayden quickly learned Gail knew her job inside and out and was passionate about doing it right. Gail believed strongly in her secretarial ministry and felt everything should be done to the honor of God and to serve the Pastor and the members of Southside Baptist Church. While Cayden felt a bit overwhelmed, she quickly realized Gail wanted to make sure she left the ministry in capable hands and that was what she wanted too.

After a relaxed, informative tour of the buildings, the two women settled in for coffee in the kitchen to get to know one another and discuss the best way to ensure Cayden was prepared to take over the following Monday. They agreed the first order of business would be to fill her in on the backgrounds and likes/dislikes of Pastor Harwell and Youth Pastor Garrett. With her notebook and pen ready, Cayden began taking notes as Gail willingly shared information that would be invaluable to her replacement. And, as most would do, they found themselves starting at the top – Pastor Harwell.

Greg Harwell had been called as Pastor at Southside Baptist seventeen years earlier. Prior to that, he had pastored a small Baptist church in Columbia, South Carolina. He had completed his undergraduate work at

Pensacola Christian College and received his Doctor of Philosophy in Theology and Apologetics from Liberty University. He was fifty-two years old with brown wavy hair and dark brown eyes. He and his wife of thirty years, Marietta, lived in Fredericksburg along with their daughter, Rachel, who was a senior at Spotsylvania Christian Academy. One son, Paul, was a junior at Bob Jones University in the Music Education program. Their two older sons, John and James, were both married and lived in Short Pump, just outside of Richmond. Pastor Harwell's hobbies included biking, reading, chess, football, and hunting. He was blessed to have both parents healthy and living happily in Pensacola.

Pastor, as Gail referred to him, was raised in a Christian home and accepted Christ at the age of nine. He recalls how God called him to preach at sixteen during a summer camp morning devotion about Samuel. Just as Samuel answered the call of God with "here am I," so did Greg Harwell. He loved his congregation, enjoyed teaching and shepherding them, and found happiness in their joy. He also felt their pain during grief, loneliness, and disappointment – all hallmarks of a dedicated shepherd of the flock God had given him.

Pastor enjoyed life and especially time with his wife and children. One favorite theme lately was he couldn't wait to be a grandpa – to have another little Harwell to love and nurture. Gail let Cayden know that Pastor's family came second only to God. So, unless he was tied up with something pertaining to his ministry, always find him and relay any message his family might leave. This was a very important point. If there really is such a thing as a pastor having a day off, Pastor took his on Mondays. It was a day he could try to relax and hopefully spend some time with Mrs. Harwell (who, she explained, preferred to be called Marietta).

Gail also shared some of Pastor's likes and dislikes. He liked his coffee black, drank Pepsi or Sprite but should drink more water, and didn't care for a lot of perfumes or air fresheners in the office. He expected professionalism but with a kind, gentle manner. During the week, he usually wore shirt and tie and always had a sports coat available. Appropriate dress for Cayden would be dresses, skirts and blouses, or suits.

Gail finished off this informative biographical sketch with a very important point. Greg Harwell was a great boss. Cayden should never be hesitant or fearful to talk with him.

They stopped for a break to check messages and stretch their legs before Gail gave a shorter biographical sketch of their youth pastor. Daniel Garrett was twenty-seven years old. He had come to Southside Baptist three years earlier. He held a Bachelor of Ministry from Virginia Baptist College in Fredericksburg and was a wonderful youth pastor. The children loved him, and the teens found in him a sympathetic and caring personality. His love of the outdoors was a definite plus where the teens were concerned, as he enjoyed taking them hiking, backpacking, and camping. He grew up in Charleston, South Carolina and moved to Virginia as a teen when his father took a job in Washington, DC. While Daniel enjoyed almost any sport, fishing was his favorite.

Cayden found herself wondering about the youth pastor and how he would get along with her. Gail did point out that Daniel was outgoing with the children but could seem to be a bit reserved when meeting people his own age. It was something he was working on, but she didn't want Cayden getting the wrong opinion of him if he didn't warm up to her right away. Cayden realized she would have to do her best to make sure they worked well together. It sounded like they might not have a lot in common but that really didn't matter. They both loved the Lord and that was the important thing – anything else could be worked through over time.

They were surprised to look at the clock and realize it was almost one o'clock. No wonder Cayden's stomach was beginning to growl. She'd been careful not to eat a lot of breakfast just in case nerves kicked in over the morning. Gail invited her to lunch at a nearby Mexican restaurant and Cayden accepted immediately. They enjoyed their meals, Gail's treat, and returned to the office ready to start on the next phase of training. Cayden realized she had a lot to learn but also that she had a great teacher. Gail took her time to explain things and shared her notes eagerly, which was a true blessing for Cayden. Later, she would incorporate her own notes with Gail's and have a quite comprehensive set of guidelines, tips, and general information.

The week progressed and by Wednesday Cayden was handling many duties with minor suggestions from Gail. She had spent some time with Pastor during which he outlined his expectations and goals for his staff. This was very informative and helpful to round out everything she'd already learned.

On Thursday, her Sunday school teacher, Jeff Carson, stopped by to show her how she would assist him in his capacity as church Treasurer. She would mainly keep several spreadsheets updated and mail out checks with correspondence as needed. It was a good chance for her to get to know Jeff better. His class on Sunday had been fun and insightful. Anyone could tell he had spent time studying and preparing for the class and that he loved doing it. She was going to enjoy working with him as well as being one of his students.

Before Jeff left that afternoon, he extended an invitation from his wife, Teresa, to join them for dinner Friday evening. Each night Cayden had gone home almost too tired to even stop by a fast-food restaurant, but she was excited to accept the invitation. He gave her the address of their farmhouse in Stafford and let her know to dress casually and be prepared to quite possibly play a board game or two. Gail chimed in that Cayden had better be ready because the Carson clan was known to be quite competitive. This only made Friday night more fun to contemplate as she drove home. In fact, she was feeling so good she stopped by a mom-and-pop diner, went inside, and sat down for a lovely supper of fried chicken and mashed potatoes. Her first week in her new job was almost done, she had plans for a fun Friday night, and she could sleep late Saturday! God was definitely good!!

All too soon, Cayden's week of training was complete, and she had tearfully bid her trainer and new friend goodbye. Gail and Anthony were packed up and would be leaving for Nags Head early Saturday morning. Armed with her copious notes and Gail's cell phone number, she found herself ready for her job to really begin the following week.

# Chapter 7

Cayden arrived at the office early Monday morning so that she would feel settled before the workday began. She had stopped by Starbucks on the way in and came to the office with her peppermint mocha and breakfast sandwich. With Pastor Harwell off today, she would spend most of the day alone and her plan was to enjoy breakfast while reviewing email, checking voicemail, and making final tweaks to her notes.

A little after nine o'clock, a chime announced someone had come in the side door. She knew that whoever it was had a keycard, which meant it wasn't a visitor. Also, they obviously liked to whistle, and they were headed her way. Before she could come around her desk, a young man sauntered into the office balancing McDonald's coffee, a briefcase, and a suit bag. When he saw Cayden, his whistling stopped, and the coffee cup almost flew from his hand. He was obviously surprised to see her – almost as surprised as she was at his appearance.

Being a newcomer to her job and the church, she would need to navigate carefully when greeting visitors to the office. She didn't want to offend a church member by welcoming them to the church they had attended for ten years. So, she opted to introduce herself and see where that took her.

"Hi, I'm Cayden Dewitt, the new church secretary." There, she thought, that sounded friendly and informative.

The young man managed to set the coffee cup on the corner of her desk and extend his hand to Cayden. "They told me you would be Gail's replacement. I guess I wasn't thinking you would have started yet. That's my office over there – the one that says 'Daniel Garrett, Youth Pastor.' Nice to meet you." He quickly picked up his coffee, went into his office and closed the door.

Thinking he would return and strike up a get-to-know-you conversation, Cayden waited at the corner of her desk. When he didn't come back out of his office, she sat down and continued her breakfast all the while wondering about what she considered sort of odd behavior when meeting a new co-worker. Should she take the first step, knock on his door, and see where it took them? After all, she supposed he was in a way one of her bosses. Maybe that was something she needed to confirm with Gail or Pastor. In the meantime, she decided to let it go and get back to work. After all, he had to walk by her desk to leave the office. She could try to converse with him then.

Daniel was taken aback by the appearance of an attractive young woman standing in the office. During his vacation, Pastor had emailed him concerning Gail's situation and the new secretary. He just hadn't given any thought to what the new secretary would look like or her age. In fact, the little that had flitted through his mind pictured the replacement as a woman around the same age as Gail. Boy was that wrong! He had meandered into the office in his own world, looking forward to getting back into a workday routine, and there stood this lovely creature with hints of red in her hair and blue eyes the color of the sky on a summer's day. In just the moment they interacted, he noted her long lashes and a few freckles across her nose. So, what did he do? He awkwardly introduced himself and practically ran into his office – where he remained for the next hour. All his life, he had struggled with being uncomfortable around new people. To compensate, he either threw caution to the wind and said whatever he thought, or he remained silent. The former often made him appear juvenile and sometimes uncaring. But remaining silent came across as aloof and that meant missing out on a lot of opportunities. This was especially true for the ministry God had called him to, which was not just to be a youth pastor but to one day pastor a church.

Daniel had grown up in a Christian home and accepted Christ at age eleven. As a young teen, his family toured the Holy Land, and it was there he knew God was calling him into full-time ministry. He surrendered his life to God at a sunrise service at the Sea of Galilee.

The last three years, with Pastor as his mentor, he had settled into his position as youth pastor. Southside members treated him like a son or brother, and he was always being invited into homes for meals and often casseroles were delivered to the single youth pastor. Sometimes, he caught a glimpse of a possible ulterior motive when the mothers praised the cooking or baking skills of their unmarried daughters. But he couldn't complain because the meals were delicious, and the subtle hints were pretty easily sidestepped. Growing up with three older sisters helped in this respect. He recognized pitfalls and knew how the female of the species operated – at least he thought he did.

Then, why was he hiding in his office? This woman had only stated her name and job title and he was hiding from her. Best to start out as he intended to go. Cayden (that was the name she said, right?) was just another pretty girl and she was a co-worker he would be around a lot. He needed to do what the sign on his desk said and *suck it up, buttercup!*

He had come to the office dressed in sweats with the intention to change into his normal work attire, shirt and tie, after his first cup of coffee. So, he quickly changed before venturing forth from his office.

On the pretense of going for more coffee, he took his empty cup and walked out into the open office area where Cayden's desk sat. She was busy typing, but he was determined to break the ice. "I'm heading to the kitchen for a fresh cup of coffee. Can I get you one? Of course, it won't measure up to Starbucks but then again it won't cost five dollars. You know that five dollars could really help a kid in Africa." Realizing what he'd just said, he practically ran from the room before she had time to speak. Instead of putting his best foot forward, he'd stuck his size elevens firmly into his mouth. Insulting her for spending her own money on coffee instead of giving it to missions was not a way to make friends. It wasn't even a way to speak to a stranger you never planned to meet again. All the while he was in the kitchen, he debated if he should just scurry back to his office and stay put the rest of the day or if he should try to repair this current fiasco. Scurrying had definite advantages but wouldn't help anything. Therefore, trying to fix the situation was the best plan but how to do it?

If his sisters had taught him nothing else, it was that most women really like chocolate. So, he scrounged around his pockets for change and perused the chocolate selection in the vending machine. There it was in all its shining splendor – a Peppermint Patty – sweet, fragrant and ten cents more than he had on him. Thinking over his options, he remembered seeing some change in the coffee concession box. Justifying his actions that he could borrow a dime and put it back later, he began shaking the acrylic box to try and dislodge the needed dime. At the same time the dime fell out of the box, he realized someone was standing behind him. Knowing who it was but hoping it wasn't, Daniel turned around to find Cayden intently watching him. No way could he explain he was getting money to buy her a gift to apologize for his earlier rude comment. Instead, he placed the dime back in the box and retreated to his office. What a day this was turning out to be and it wasn't even noon.

Cayden was dumbfounded by Daniel's remark concerning the cost of her coffee and the hint she should quit buying Starbucks and give the money instead to missions. When he'd come out of his office and asked about getting her a cup of coffee, she thought this was a good icebreaker and a way to start a friendly conversation. But that was not to be. And, to make matters worse, she walked in on him taking money out of the concession box. Gail had explained that money from the concession was donated monthly to a different missionary. So, seeing Daniel borrowing money from the box made Cayden think Gail's assessment of this man might be a bit skewed. Luckily, she only had to work with him but for the time being, it was going to be awkward. Shaking her head, she returned to her desk and got back to work.

Daniel decided that he should treat Cayden like one of the teens. He had no problem with them. He could put together whole, understandable sentences without insulting them. He could even hold his own in an entire conversation, which meant it was possible to fix things and get on with his day. When he returned to the office, Cayden didn't look up from her computer keyboard. Even when he cleared his throat, she continued typing. This called for more direct measures.

Determined to fix things, he asked, "Cayden, could we start over again? I seem to be putting my foot in my mouth and making a terrible first impression." Still no response.

"Hello, my name is Daniel Garrett and it's so lovely to make your acquaintance. I look forward to working with you and am available to help if you ever need anything. Welcome to Fredericksburg and to Southside Baptist." This brought her gaze to meet his and he saw a very faint smile play across her face. Okay, this was maybe going to work. Now, if she'd just say something so he didn't have to keep talking.

"Nice to meet you, Daniel. Gail told me a lot about you and how much she thinks of you. Thank you for the warm welcome." She'd said that with a straight face but still no real warmth. The whole borrowing money from the concession box was probably a huge contributor to that.

39

"As co-workers and hopefully friends, I would like to apologize for a couple of things to clear the air. My comment about your Starbucks coffee wasn't meant as an insult. I just get a bit uncomfortable with new people and wind up saying the wrong thing. The incident you witnessed in the kitchen was in part your fault." Daniel finished this statement with a grimace, realizing it would probably be taken as yet another insult. Relief washed over him as she smiled, and he found himself mesmerized by her.

"You're as bad as my brother, Carter, but he's only sixteen and just learning how to have grown-up conversations!" Now, she was laughing, and he couldn't help joining in at the pure absurdity of the situation.

Quickly, he apologized again. "I'm sorry for what I said. I had decided to make a peace offering of chocolate candy but came up a dime short. When you walked in, I was borrowing the dime from the concession box with the full intention of repaying it later this morning. Unfortunately, I'm sure the whole fiasco has left you thinking you'll be working with a dimwitted, immature, rude thief. Please forgive me and tell me how to fix all this."

He must have looked sincere enough because she smiled and offered a solution. "Chocolate candy, huh? That would do the trick. Maybe you could take your own money back to the kitchen and try again?"

Taking this as his cue to escape unscathed and fix everything, he quickly retrieved change from his desk and returned to the kitchen. After buying the Peppermint Patty, he placed any leftover change in the concession box to make up for his previous misdemeanor. Chocolate in hand, Daniel returned to the office and presented the candy to Cayden.

"It is with sincere apologies that I offer this candy as restitution for any previous insults or misdeeds. Please eat it in good health. And now I'm returning to my office before something else in the idiotic realm escapes my mouth." On that, he fled to his office but this time with a lighter heart. They were going to work together for a long time hopefully and they could get to know each other as time went by. For now, it was good just to feel on an even keel with her.

Cayden was glad Daniel had made the effort to clear the air. From this morning's antics (that was the best word she could think to describe all that had transpired), he was probably very popular with the children and teens. In that respect, he reminded her of Carter, which should endear him to her; but all it did was make her realize she didn't need or want another brother. While Carter was funny and she enjoyed her time with him, she often was the object of his teasing and good-humored antics, which sometimes irritated and embarrassed her. If Daniel proved to fall in that same category, she wasn't sure their relationship would ever be classified as "friends." She would be satisfied if they just got along well as co-workers. Her new job was important – so, she would do her part to make sure that happened.

# Chapter 8

 uly Fourth holiday fell on a Tuesday and Pastor decided that in addition to the holiday his staff could also take Monday off. This gave Cayden a nice long, four-day weekend, which meant a trip home. She was as excited as a kid at Christmas. She had only made a quick trip to visit her family once since moving and she was more than ready for a long talk with her mother and some home cooking. It would also give her a chance to bring back some items that would prove useful in the apartment. She might even have time to reconnect with old friends.

Over the last month, she had met a lot of people and made some friends. However, she hadn't really fell into any sort of routine of visiting or going out with anyone just to relax and have fun. Her time seemed focused on work, which was totally understandable since all of this was new to her, but it did leave a small void that being back home with family and lifelong friends would help fill for a few days.

When Cayden called her mom with the good news, she was surprised to learn her family was leaving the next day for a ten-day mission trip to Texas. A missionary responsible for distributing gospel tracts just over the border into Mexico had put out a request for people to share the gospel during a festival where thousands of people would attend. Her parents and even Carter had volunteered. Feeling like a deflated balloon, Cayden decided going home without her family there wouldn't be the same.

With a new resolve, she called Ila Bennett to see if she had plans for Saturday. Ila had been working out of town for the last three weeks but was due to arrive home on Friday. When the call went straight to voicemail,

Cayden left a message and hung up. Her next thought was maybe Allie would be up for getting together. When Allie answered her call, Cayden knew immediately that her new friend was not well.

"Oh, Cayden, I would love to get together but I went to the doctor yesterday and have tested positive for flu. Can you believe it? Right here in mid-summer and I have flu! Whoever heard of such a thing?" A sneeze followed Allie's response and effectively put an end to their conversation. Cayden assured Allie she would be praying for her before ending the call.

Don and Beth Mahoney were on a motorcoach tour of New England for another week. Ellen came to mind, but Cayden quickly recalled she was visiting family in Ireland for the first two weeks of July. She couldn't think of anyone else who might be available on short notice.

For the last four years, Cayden had been surrounded with young people running here and there, always ready to find something fun or interesting to do, which meant she had spent very little time alone. But now was a very different time and it was up to her to make the best of a wonderful opportunity to maybe even make a new friend or just to spend time getting acquainted with the city she now called home. On that note, Cayden spent the next hour checking out what Spotsylvania County had to offer and came up with a game plan. She was going sightseeing!

She had lived in Fredericksburg for a month but hadn't yet ventured into old downtown. So, her plan for Saturday started with exploring the shops and eateries in this historic city – along with what seemed like thousands of others making the most of their holiday weekend. After grabbing a map at the visitor's center, she made her way along Caroline Street. Deciding to just take a leisurely approach to her day, she wandered through antique and vintage clothes shops, and trendy gift shops. Like a true tourist, she took photos of the old churches with their impressive spires and the lovely architecture. She particularly found interesting the alleyways between historic buildings that had been transformed into lovely courtyards. Surprisingly, the crown jewel for her sightseeing/shopping trip was Goolrick's Pharmacy, which had been in business since the late 1800's. She felt as if she'd taken a step back in time upon entering the store and instantly fell in love with the old-fashioned soda fountain. Luckily, it was lunchtime and warranted the purchase of a chicken salad sandwich on toasted bread and a cherry cola, which came with a paper (not plastic) straw. This completed her first morning of a long weekend with a happy feeling of adventure and a little feeling of belonging. One thing was for sure – she would be back soon to try one of their signature milkshakes!

On the way back to her car, Cayden decided to come back in a few months when the leaves were changing and take a carriage tour of downtown. She also wanted to tour the historic buildings at another time that might not be so busy. To round out her day, she decided to meander through the mall and maybe even treat herself to a movie. This city, her new city, was growing on her. Even so, she found herself wishing she had someone to share all this with but was sure that would come in time. She just needed to be patient, something that wasn't her favorite thing to be.

Sunday morning was glorious. With temperatures predicted to be in the nineties later in the day, Cayden decided to take a run before church and enjoy the coolness of home in the afternoon. After a quick shower, she grabbed her Bible and arrived in plenty of time for Sunday school. She made her way to the fellowship hall where people were mingling and enjoying pastries before class. After speaking to several people, she sat down to enjoy a doughnut and juice and was joined by Daniel, who looked a bit disheveled for a Sunday morning.

"Is everything okay? Your tie is crooked, and you look like you haven't slept," she asked with concern.

"Well, one of the teens had to have emergency surgery to remove his appendix early this morning and I've been at the hospital with his parents. Just had time to change clothes and fly to get here," he explained as he took a deep breath, seeming to calm down a little.

"Is he okay? Is there anything I can do for the family or for you?" She was instantly aware that assistance might be needed and wanted to do whatever she could.

"That's why I'm here. Could you teach the seven-year-old class? The teen is Billy Thompson and his mom, Renee, teaches that class but, of course, she wants to stay with Billy. The lesson is about Daniel and the lion's den. I have the teacher's book and everything you'll need right here." He offered her a packet, which contained cutouts, memory verses, and the promised teacher's book.

"Of course, I'll do my best." She was answering even as she scanned the notes Mrs. Thompson had made about the lesson. "Now, you need to take a minute to collect yourself, straighten your tie, and get to class. I'll round up the seven-year-olds."

As he was walking away, Cayden called out, "Daniel, I'm sure the Thompsons were so grateful you were there with them. Your heart for others shows through your actions – that's impressive." She wasn't sure but even though he didn't turn around, it looked as if his shoulders straightened, and his step was less hurried. She walked away thinking that maybe this semi-annoying boy/man would make a great pastor one day.

After worship service, Cayden took care of a few things in her office before deciding a holiday weekend called for something more than a fast-food lunch. Something more in line with a true Sunday dinner was calling her name and she knew just the place to get it. A few miles south was a great restaurant with home-cooked meals and she set out to enjoy one. As she walked in the door, the realization struck that a lot of others had the same idea. She was just about to turn around and leave when she heard someone call her name. Surprised, she looked around and saw Daniel sitting alone in a booth waving her over. As she approached, he stood up and invited her to join him.

"Hey, I saw you walking up and knew the line would be too long for most people to wait," he said motioning to the crowd waiting for a table.

"Which leads me to wonder how you got here early enough to already be seated. Did you skip church?" Knowing full well he hadn't, she couldn't resist teasing him.

Grinning at the thought, he indicated the *Reserved* sign on the table. "My cousin owns this place and always saves me a table unless I tell him I have other Sunday dinner plans. There are perks to having family nearby."

"Well, thank you for sharing your table with me. Are you expecting anyone else? I guess I always think of you having some places to go after church. You're always so popular, especially with the singles crowd and their mamas." She couldn't help the last part of that statement because she had noticed that some of the single women and their mothers seemed to show him extra attention. It was something Ila and Allie liked to tease him about too.

Turning a little red, he replied, "You've noticed that, huh? That's one reason I like a standing Sunday dinner invitation. It makes it easier and keeps me from having to come up with excuses." She couldn't help but laugh while also realizing the logic behind his planning.

Dinner was enjoyable, with good food and a surprisingly comfortable conversation. They exchanged information on their backgrounds and families. As they discussed college days, they even discovered a couple of acquaintances in common. Even though he was six years her senior, Cayden found him a nice dinner companion. He only reminded her of an annoying brother once or twice.

"I thought you had big plans for the long weekend," she mentioned as their entrees arrived. "Did something happen?"

"I had planned to spend a couple of days camping and hiking, but the weather forecast didn't look too promising. That meant regrouping, which meant taking care of things around the house." He grimaced at that thought before continuing. "I'm glad it worked out that way though because I was able to be with Billy and his family when they needed me. Hopefully, I'll get to kayak tomorrow morning early before the heat sets in and the thunderstorms arrive."

"It's funny you mention kayaking. I planned to go home for the holiday and bring my kayak back with me. When I found out my family had volunteered to join a mission's trip to Texas, going home suddenly wasn't so appealing. I'll bring it back next time. Don and Beth said I could store it along with their kayaks behind the garage." Even she could hear the wistfulness in her voice. Kayaking would have been fun to do over the long holiday weekend.

After a drink of tea, Daniel suggested. "Maybe you'd like to join me tomorrow. I have two kayaks and all the gear. Since storms are forecast, the planned route won't take that long but it should be good exercise, and we should see some cool sights."

"Are you sure? Because I hadn't thought about what I would do tomorrow and getting out on the water would be fun." She smiled as she thought about joining him for an excursion. "But no antics like my brother would be prone to do. Carter threw a rubber snake into my kayak and he nearly got his head knocked off for that stunt."

"No, I can assure you I take water safety – in fact safety in general but especially in sports – very seriously. Otherwise, the teens would always be trying to top me and that would not be good. In fact, see this scar?" He pulled his hair back to expose a scar on his right temple. "I pulled a similar stunt with my oldest sister only it was a real snake, and she did bean me. Of course, she was immediately scared half to death because she had made her baby brother cry and that was a no-no. However, in that instance, my dad only agreed with her retaliation. Never did that again."

After sharing a few other kayaking stories, they came up with a plan for meeting at six o'clock the next morning. She only had to bring bottled water and a snack. They would be off the water well before noon and could grab lunch at his favorite barbecue place if that suited her.

The rest of their meal was spent with more conversation and laughter, and Cayden realized for the first time that this co-worker could very well become a nice friend. At the same time, to his astonishment, Daniel realized he might be in trouble where this young woman was concerned. Strangely enough, he didn't mind.

The kayaking trip went well, and Cayden loved the barbecue they had for lunch. Afterwards, they went their separate ways, but an easy alliance had been made that would go a long way for them as co-workers and perhaps for building some type of friendship.

# Chapter 9

After the July Fourth weekend, things settled into a normal routine of work, church, occasional outings, and a few trips home. Cayden often found herself restless without being able to explain even to herself what was lacking. On her last trip home, she had discussed this with her mother, who understood her daughter better than anyone – Cayden was lonely for close friends and for purpose. Even as a child, she relished close kinship with a few special friends, and she was always looking for something to do.

Looking into her daughter's eyes, she asked, "Have you made any close ties, made friends with whom you can share your heart?"

Without hesitation, Cayden replied, "Not close ties. You know I love Beth and Ellen, but they're older and move in somewhat different circles. I am forging friendships with Ila and Allie, but their jobs spill over into their 'free' time more than mine does. And to be honest, I guess I haven't tried to deepen those relationships. It's only been two months and I'm afraid to seem needy."

"Ah, your fear is getting in the way and believe me I get that," her mom responded. "But you know the saying 'to make a friend, you must show yourself friendly.' I know it's hard to come into a new situation and try to decipher existing friendships and determine where you might fit in. Think back to when you first met Marta, a stranger you were assigned to share a room with, a girl so different from you at first glance. Now, even though you're still different, you're close like sisters and that took a bit of work."

Smiling, Cayden recalled how the first month was most interesting because both girls were used to having their own bathroom at home. Suddenly, they were sharing one small bedroom and a tiny bathroom. After some grimaces and muttering under their breath, they realized they had to talk and come to an agreement on how to move forward. They worked at it and learned to graciously live together in peace for the most part. Over time, their friendship truly became more of a sisterhood that would stand the test of time and distance.

"So, you're saying I'm the new kid on the block, and I need to try harder if, indeed, I want to have close friends instead of just people I go to church with and occasionally hang out with." Cayden recognized that her mother did what she had always done before. She listened, saw the problem, laid it out for Cayden to see and patiently waited for her daughter to work it out. "Okay, I promise to try harder and to not be afraid. I feel sure the groundwork is there for a great friendship with Ila and Allie. I just need to do my part, but you must promise to do your part too."

"And what might that be, daughter mine?" Meg asked in surprise.

"Pray, Mama, pray!" was Cayden's quick reply.

Now, it was up to Cayden to put her plan into action. It was Thursday night, and she had no plans for the weekend. Maybe the girls didn't either. Anyway, it was worth a try to see if she could get something going. Like Meg said, she needed to show herself friendly.

As she picked up her phone to call Ila, a call came across from Allie, who wondered if Cayden was busy Friday night. She and Ila were planning a girls' game night and invited her to join them. By the end of the call, plans were in place for the three girls to meet at Ila's townhouse Friday after work. They would order Chinese food and play board games and maybe even Mario Kart. Everyone would bring their favorite snacks and soda or juice. Cayden realized her prayers (and her mom's) were working.

Game night was a bit more competitive than Cayden thought it would be, but she was up for it. At the Dewitt house, games weren't just for fun they were a chance for victory! Letting her guard down was easy as soon as Ila brought Scrabble out and they started to play. Nobody beat her at Scrabble – that is until Allie scored a Bingo which just so happened to include a triple word score.

At the end of the evening, they all agreed to make girls' game night at least a monthly must. As the evening wound down, there was more food and idle talk that turned into friendly sharing of concerns, dreams, desires. All three wanted to please the Lord and all three agreed they had always prayed for a godly husband but in God's timing. Ila admitted to praying more earnestly lately for a husband and she even went so far as to admit she would really love it if that man was a preacher. Cayden shared her desire to make friends and to find God's purpose for her life. Allie asked for prayer that she be more outgoing, to get past her shyness. After prayer and hugs, the party dispersed. Before going to bed, Cayden texted her mom and thanked her for praying – it was working.

As church secretary, Cayden helped with different things in the church. So, when Ellen asked her to help plan an all-day ladies' fellowship, it wasn't a chore. In fact, it was an honor and a joy. This was right up her alley, and she knew working with Ellen would be a blast. The fellowship would be in mid-October, which gave them two months to get ready, and they jumped into planning mode with both feet. Their ladies' group held brainstorming meetings, made notes, created spreadsheets, and had the time of their lives. Sub-committees were formed, and duties were assigned so that everyone had a part and the fellowship would be all the sweeter for it. After one long meeting, Cayden was getting ready for bed when she realized how far God had brought her in a short time to be a part of her church ladies' group and making lasting friendships. He was also using her and that made her heart sing. Another late-night text went out to Meg – keep praying, mom, please never stop!

During all this, an unexpected friendship was forming. Don and Beth's home sat on three acres, which meant neighbors were not close. Most of the neighbors Cayden had met were in passing as she jogged or saw them in a store or restaurant. That changed somewhat on a Saturday morning in late September when their nearest neighbor knocked on her door.

Paula Benton owned the ten-acre farmette behind Don and Beth. Cayden had met Paula once and understood that her elderly mother, Virginia Lampton, lived with her. Mrs. Virginia had been diagnosed with dementia two years earlier, at which time Paula became her primary caretaker. It had taken only a short while to realize Mrs. Virginia couldn't live alone any longer and Paula invited her mother to live with her.

It took Cayden by surprise when she opened the door and Paula was frantically looking around, sort of like a lost child might appear. When she spoke, Paula focused on her and explained that she had tried Beth and Don, but no one answered and that she needed help.

"My mother has fallen, and I can't help her up. I was hoping Don was home. What should I do?" she asked a surprised Cayden. She looked as if she might faint from distress and the exertion of looking for help.

"I can come but we should call 911," Cayden replied as she grabbed a jacket. "Is she conscious? Is she bleeding?"

"I got so excited I just jumped in the golf cart and cut a path through the field. She is conscious and isn't bleeding but I need to get back to her," she said over her shoulder as she went down the steps. "Can you call 911?"

Cayden called 911 as she was following Paula and jumped into the golf cart driver seat. When they arrived at the house, Mrs. Virginia was sitting up but could not pull herself up onto a chair or the sofa. Cayden soothed both ladies and advised that Mrs. Virginia shouldn't move but to just sit still because help was on the way. By the time the rescue squad arrived, everyone was calmer, and Mrs. Virginia even remembered what had happened. As she put it, she had decided to get a glass of water from the kitchen and her feet just got tangled up and she fell. The paramedics were able to check her over to ascertain there were no broken bones and to help her onto a stretcher. Paula was upset that they wanted to take her mother to the hospital until Cayden volunteered to drive her there and stay with her. She waited with Paula until Mrs. Virginia had been checked over and discharged. Together, she and Paula were able to take Mrs. Virginia home and get her into bed.

From that time, Paula and Cayden began forging a friendship, which surprised Beth and Don because Paula had no use for *Bible thumpers* (what she called Christians). She put up with them out of necessity but didn't want to hear anything about God or church. Cayden began praying earnestly for Paula and Mrs. Virginia because they needed Christ but also because they needed healing and rest from burdens that accompany dementia patients and their caregivers.

Yet a third text went out to Meg – Thanks, mom, for always praying and for always knowing what I need! This was followed a little later with a phone conversation to explain the situation and to say Cayden finally felt needed in her new circumstances. God was so gracious, and He had only just begun working in Cayden's heart to ready it for things yet to come.

# Chapter 10

*I*t was the first Sunday in November, and Cayden was excited to hear the evangelist who was to be present his ministry at the morning service. Pastor had given her a brief thumbnail sketch of his testimony for the bulletin last week and it had intrigued her. She knew just enough to make her want to hear him fill in the blanks. The part about him coming out of homclessness was particularly interesting since she couldn't begin to understand how that could happen or how God could use it to bless someone. As she dressed for church, her mind kept going back to the idea.

The evangelist, Phillip Doucet, was at church when Cayden arrived. Even though she always arrived early to make sure everything was running smoothly, he was already in the vestibule greeting everyone coming in the front door. Her first thoughts were that he wasn't as old as she thought he would be, and he didn't look like any homeless person she'd ever seen. In fact, he was probably only in his mid-thirties. He wasn't tall but he wasn't short either, and the way he carried himself indicated he'd been in the military at some point. But what was most noticeable, even at a quick glance, was the ease with which he interacted with people and his ability to make them feel welcome. After introducing herself and asking if there was anything she could do to assist him, Phillip quickly assured her he had everything he needed.

"I overestimated how long it would take to get here from home and arrived earlier than planned. That gave me time for a quick detour to McDonald's for a sweet tea and sausage biscuit and still got me here half-hour early. But God is good in letting me meet so many of your people before

Sunday school starts." He gave her a slow grin before shaking hands with the next person entering the church.

"Oh, I'm sorry. I should have told you we have refreshments in the fellowship hall on Sundays before classes start at nine fifteen. That would have saved you the trip to McDonald's." Cayden was kicking herself for not including that information when Phillip's words stopped her negative train of thought.

"No problem. I met some nice folks while I was in line and got to share the gospel with them and invite them to church. I'm praying they show up." Phillip's face almost glowed when he mentioned witnessing to the people.

"Great! Pastor said you're going to share some of your testimony with the young adult class during Sunday school. Shall I show you where they meet?" Taking his nod as agreement, Cayden began walking down the hall to the annex. "We're all excited to learn more about your ministry. Southside has been considering a program to help the homeless in our city. From what I've read about *Feed My Sheep* and the impact it has had in other places, I think you'll find a very interested audience."

They chatted as they made their way to the room where her class met. Several people were already in the room, drinking coffee and catching up with each other. Ila and Allie came in with their teacher, Jeff Carson, in time to join the introductions.

"Phillip, we're glad you could join us today. Do you need audiovisual equipment set up?" Jeff shook Phillip's hand as he offered his assistance.

"No, it's just me and my story. Hopefully, that will be enough," Phillip answered with a chuckle. "How many do you usually have in your class?"

Jeff laughed as he told Phillip, "We run between fifteen to twenty, and most of them are about your age. That will make it more interesting to them. I know I'm looking forward to learning more about you and your program. My wife, Teresa, and I have been working with the Salvation Army for the last year and have been praying for Southside to start its own program to help the homeless people here."

As the room began to fill up, Cayden took her seat beside Ila, who was uncharacteristically quiet. When she looked at her friend, she noticed that Ila hadn't taken her eyes off Phillip. "Are you okay? Do you know Phillip?" She gave Ila's hand a squeeze and saw that her friend looked almost dazed.

"No, I don't know him. I just wasn't expecting the 'evangelist with a story' to tell to be around my age. Nor did I think he would be so handsome. Do you know if he's married?" Ila was nothing if not direct.

"The short bio of Phillip that Pastor gave me for the bulletin didn't mention a wife or family, and he's not wearing a ring." Cayden continued to watch her friend and wonder at her reaction to a man she'd never met before.

"Well, I think we need to find out a bit more about Mr. Doucet. Maybe we should invite him to lunch." Never one to be shy or hesitant, Ila jumped in with both feet when she was curious about something or someone. But this time it might be a bit hasty to jump without more information.

"Pastor has invited him home for lunch. Let's hold off on that thought for just a bit. After all, if the church decides to become part of his *Feed My Sheep* ministry, we'll have plenty of opportunity to get to know Phillip better." Cayden finished speaking just as Jeff called the class to order and opened in prayer. Today really was going to prove interesting in many ways.

After Sunday school, Phillip spoke with each class member as they headed in different directions. Ila would have kept talking with him if Cayden hadn't pulled her out the door and down the hall to the choir room for practice. Not seeming to notice, Phillip joined Pastor Harwell and continued greeting newcomers until the service began and he moved up front. After several songs, announcements, and the offering, Pastor introduced Phillip and turned the service over to him.

"If you're like most folks, you're thinking that I'm sort of young to be an evangelist. I am thirty-five years old. But what I lack in years' experience, I've more than made up in life experience. So, here's my story in a condensed version. I accepted Christ at the age of twelve. My parents were relatively new Christians, but they made sure we were at Sunday services and participated in many of the youth functions. After high school, I became a lineman for Duke Energy in Raleigh. I joined the Army in 2001 right after 9/11. During the eight years I was in the Army, I did two tours in Iraq. The last tour closed out my military career and I returned to my parents' home in North Carolina just before Christmas 2009. But nothing seemed to fit – my civilian clothes, my old friends, my mindset. To put it plainly, I didn't fit, and I had no clue how to fix it. On January 10, 2010, I told my mother I was going for a walk. After about two hours, she started texting asking when I'd be home. When I didn't reply, she started calling. By dark, I'd been walking for seven hours and didn't want to stop. I called mom and told her not to worry (that worked, right, ladies?) and promised to call each week. I threw my cell phone in the trash and kept walking. I had no plan, no destination, no idea why this felt right. By the time my cash ran out and my only credit card was maxed out, I had walked or begged rides to Washington, DC. I became one of the throngs of homeless people in that city, and I did not care." Phillip stopped to let his words sink in before continuing.

"There are many organizations in DC that help the homeless – civic organizations, churches, government agencies. One church offered free transportation to the church Friday evenings for a free meal and on Sunday afternoons for a service and a meal. I usually didn't go to any of the church services, but the temperatures one Sunday in June made an air-conditioned van look very inviting. So, I climbed on board, attended the service, and ate a good meal. As everyone was getting back in the van, a young man named Ben came up and asked if I'd like to be his guest at the YMCA for a workout and a swim. Being in the Army and living on the streets teaches you to read people quickly. Ben seemed on the up and up and going to the Y meant a free shower. So, I took him up on his offer. As we rode to the Y, Ben explained how his invitation came about."

"That morning as he was leaving for church, God impressed on him to bring his gym bag and throw in an extra pair of trunks and a change of clothes. During the morning services and while serving the meal, he didn't give it another thought until he felt compelled to offer the invitation to me. At the Y, I showered, swam, and worked out and left wearing a new (to me) pair of shorts and a t-shirt. As Ben took me back to the park where I stayed during the days, he didn't ask questions and I didn't offer information. He just told me about his life and how he had come to know the Lord. When I got out of the car, he promised that if I came again next Sunday, we could go to the Y again."

"The following week, I was digging through some trash and found a discarded Bible. With nothing better to do, I started reading in Matthew and read through Revelation. By Sunday, I was ready to go back to church and this time I listened. Ben was true to his word. We went to the Y again just like the week before but this time I was ready to talk and ask questions."

"The services and meals were nice but what Ben did by giving of himself and by acknowledging me as a person was phenomenal. As long as I was one of many in a homeless shelter or at a service for homeless people, I could hide and feel insulated. But once Ben allowed God to direct his paths to minister to my needs and see me as a person who matters, I once again became Phillip Doucet, a man who had accepted Christ so long ago. The Holy Spirit flooded my soul with love so great I fell to my knees with my head on the floor and stayed there for what seemed like hours crying like a newborn baby." Phillip paused and the sanctuary was quiet.

"I know my story sounds a bit like the prodigal son, and there are a lot of similarities. Thank the Lord, in my story, there was a godly man who had no vested interest in Phillip Doucet but was willing to put actions to his faith, which made all the difference."

"Ben introduced me to his pastor and later that week the church bought me a bus ticket home. I'd called my parents each week as promised but this call was the one call they'd been praying for. They picked me up at the bus station, took me home where I think I ate the whole fatted calf, and listened to my story. With my parents' help and assistance from Uncle Sam, I enrolled at Pensacola Christian College and graduated in 2014. During my junior year, God laid a burden on my heart for the homeless population of this country. I talked with several professors and pastors, did a lot of praying, and in January 2014 the *Feed My Sheep* ministry was officially organized. That's why I'm here today."

"*Feed My Sheep* is a non-profit ministry that works with local churches to serve and aid the homeless people in their communities. The ministry has several levels of commitment starting at serving meals to hosting special services to offering shelter, all ministering not just to the physical but to the spiritual needs of each individual. It's a commitment of time, money, and love. I've traveled mostly up and down the east coast so far talking with congregations and helping them learn to effectively minister to these individuals who need so much but ask for so little. Your pastor has indicated there is a desire in your church family to join *Feed My Sheep*. My friend, Ben, is an example of what one person can do to affect positive change when they follow God's lead. My prayer is that you will become ambassadors for Christ as a beacon of His love to the homeless in Spotsylvania and Stafford counties." Phillip nodded to Pastor Harwell and left the platform.

As Cayden listened to Phillip's story, she felt a stirring in her heart for this ministry. She laughed as the thought flitted through her mind – mom must be praying overtime!

# Chapter 11

Thanksgiving was a wonderful time with family and friends. Cayden enjoyed Meg's cooking Thursday morning through Sunday dinner. And, when she packed the car to head back home, a cooler with leftovers was in the backseat and a bag of her favorite pumpkin cookies were in an open container on the passenger seat. Life was good.

She had just bypassed Richmond when Marta called. They hadn't seen each other since Memorial Day but talked or messaged regularly. After all, it seemed impossible to live with someone for four years and walk away after graduation. Their friendship was too important to both girls.

"So, are you on the way back to Fredericksburg? Thanksgiving was good?" Marta inquired of her best friend. "I can almost bet you have some of your mom's baked goods in the front seat with you – my guess would be pumpkin cookies since they are the best. Am I right?"

With a mouth slightly full of cookie, Cayden owned up to the fact that Marta knew her better than anyone and that yes, indeed, pumpkin cookies were riding shotgun. "Just wish you were here to share one. I could really use a good face-to-face catch up with you."

"Good to know because in addition to asking about your holiday I wanted to see if you'd be interested in meeting at Tyson's Corner Center Saturday for a day of shopping. We could meet at ten o'clock at Bloomingdales," Marta offered, knowing full well it would take a lot to make Cayden decline a day of shopping. The mall just outside of DC was huge and so much fun at Christmas, which was in full swing.

"You know me too well, girl! Of course, I'll meet you and not just because you said the magic word 'shopping' but because I need to see my BFF," was her enthusiastic reply. "When I get there, I'll call you, so we can find each other easily."

Marta's giggle was followed by a loud, "Yes! I knew I could count on you, and we have a lot to discuss. Want to hear some good news?"

Without missing a beat, Cayden squealed, "You're engaged, aren't you? Wade finally popped the question?"

"Calm down girl. This news isn't that big but it is significant. I've got a job!" Marta was quick to set things right.

"Oh, that is big. But one of these days Wade will finally get up the nerve to propose and he'll be the most blessed man because you will be the best wife ever. So, back to the job. I want to hear everything!"

That's all Marta needed to jump into all the details. She had accepted a position with All in for Jesus, a missions organization located in Texas. She would be Assistant Finance Director, and, more importantly, she would be moving to Texas after New Year's. While Cayden was thrilled for Marta, her heart plummeted at the thought of her best friend, confidante, and sister in Christ moving so far away.

"Oh, Marta, that's fantastic! You'll do great and what an opportunity to use your education while serving the Lord. But Texas is so far away!" she all but cried.

"Come on now, we haven't seen each other in six months but have kept up with each other's lives. Now, instead of driving a few hours to see each other, we'll catch a plane. I checked and there are non-stop flights out of Dulles and Richmond that aren't too expensive. I'm just glad to have landed something I think I'll enjoy and be good at, while also serving God. Working at the bank has been a good experience for me but I'm ready for something in my chosen field." Cayden could hear the smile in Marta's voice, and that was all that mattered.

"Does this mean you need me to help you find a place to live? You know I'm good at bargaining." Now, Marta could hear the smile in Cayden's voice, and she knew they were both remembering the near fiasco they had when looking for an apartment after their sophomore year at Liberty. They had found the perfect place within walking distance of campus, with two bedrooms and two bathrooms. An older couple had recently converted the top floor of their Victorian home into an apartment and were renting it for a great price, but Cayden believed they could do better and proceeded to work her supposed magic. Usually a good judge of others' reactions, she totally missed it with Mr. and Mrs. Johnson. Fortunately, Marta was able to call her aside and get her to take a deep breath before she blew the whole thing sky high. In the end, the Johnsons got a good laugh out of it and even conceded to reduce rent by twenty dollars a month to make Cayden feel better about her negotiating skills. The two years they lived there were beyond expectation because the Johnsons sort of adopted them into their family.

Marta's answer was quick and decisive, "Yes, I want you to help me find a place, but you will not be haggling over anything!"

Cayden agreed and soon realized they had talked all the way into Caroline County and that traffic was beginning to slow down. This meant one thing – it would soon come to a standstill before even reaching the outskirts of Fredericksburg. She updated Marta on traffic woes and ended their conversation with a promise to call as soon as she arrived at the mall Saturday morning.

Deciding to kill two birds with one stone, so to speak, Cayden took the Ladysmith exit and stopped at McDonald's for coffee. She set her mapping app to avoid highways and took backroads through Caroline County into Spotsylvania County and on to her home. As she enjoyed a cookie, coffee, and adventuring through unknown territory on a lovely fall day, she marveled at the fact she had just thought of her apartment as *home*. It had taken six months, but it had happened – Fredericksburg was her home.

Arriving at the apartment with just enough time to store leftovers in the refrigerator and freshen up, she hurried to church and slipped into the back pew just as the first song was announced. With a quick survey of the assembled group, she spotted Allie and Ila and noticed Phillip sitting with them. Tuesday night dinner with her two friends was certainly going to be interesting.

After church, Cayden caught up with the group and everyone reported a wonderful Thanksgiving had been enjoyed by all. The conversation between the girls turned to Tuesday girls' night dinner, and Cayden volunteered to host since her mother had sent home wonderful leftovers.

"I'll make a turkey casserole to go with the home-made yeast rolls and toss a salad. Also, mom made two cheesecakes so that I could bring one home with me," she was happy to report.

Phillip, who was talking with Daniel, immediately turned around and said, "Cheesecake? Did you say cheesecake? What does a fella have to do to get invited to dinner?"

Ila was quick to answer, "Oh no, buddy, Tuesday is girls' night – no fellas allowed!"

Not to be outdone and to give it another try for at least cheesecake, Phillip replied with a pitiful expression, "Daniel's asked me to do a devotion for the youth Wednesday night. Can one of you kind ladies at least bring me a small piece of cheesecake?"

As soon as Daniel realized he was sort of part of the discussion, he chimed in, "Now wait a minute – after girls' night Cayden usually brings leftovers to the office the next morning. Don't be horning in on my arrangement for great food."

"Did someone say cheesecake? I was across the aisle talking with Pastor when I distinctly heard you all discussing my favorite food," chimed in Luke, their Sunday school teacher's son. Luke was twenty-seven years old and taught history and coached basketball at Spotsylvania Christian Academy. Because he was the pre-teen class teacher on Sunday mornings, he didn't always interact a lot with the young adult group. Also, his current girlfriend attended another Baptist church and he often attended Sunday night services with her. Tonight, however, he was flying solo and was quite interested in the current debate on cheesecake.

Allie, who was most often the quiet one, reacted before anyone else could speak, "Do you guys have a special homing device or messaging system when food is involved? My brothers can't hear a thing mom or I say concerning laundry or doing dishes but mention food and they're all ears."

Everyone turned to Allie and broke into laughter before she continued, "If you want a piece of cheesecake Wednesday night, you have to take us for coffee tonight." Now, there was a moment of silence before Ila and Cayden agreed that sounded fair.

"I have a hankering for pancakes," Cayden said with a grin. "Mom was going to make them for breakfast yesterday, but Carter whined about really wanting French toast and, of course, baby boy won. So, let's go to Olaf's because they have the best breakfast on their all-day menu."

With that, the six of them agreed and a race was made to the parking lot. Within ten minutes, they were seated at a table with menus in hand. Phillip, who had never heard of Olaf's, was perusing the menu while coffee or tea was served. Ila knew better than anyone how good late-night breakfasts were at Olaf's since her days at University of Mary Washington often included long nights of study and a trip to Olaf's for sustenance. She was only too happy to help Phillip in making his choices.

After orders were placed and the group quieted down, Daniel asked a simple but very important question. "Okay, we agreed to take you to Olaf's for coffee. But who's paying for your meals?" At this, everyone burst into laughter and the matter was quickly settled. Each person would take care of their own tab, except for the coffee, of course.

When Tuesday night rolled around, the girls had so much to talk about and such fun doing it. Dinner was wonderful and the promised cheesecake was incredible. With coffee and cheesecake in hand, they settled in for a cozy chat. Again, Cayden was struck at how this apartment was now her home and these two girls were such wonderful friends. God was so good!

Top of the discussion priority list was Ila's Thanksgiving. She was happy to report that Phillip fit right in with her parents. As she was an only child, her family's Thanksgiving was usually just the three of them, which was lovely; but having Phillips join them was beyond wonderful.

Ila gave them a quick overview of the last week by simply stating, "You'll think I'm crazy, but I truly believe he's the man God has for me. Before you say anything, and I can tell you're ready to jump on that statement, you need to know how I've been praying for the last six months and even more intensely since Phillip came into my life. I have known my entire adult life, and even in my late teens, that I wanted to be a preacher's wife and I truly believe God has imprinted that desire on my heart, which means I believe he will fulfill it. When I saw Phillip that first Sunday morning, it truly was as if I heard God telling me Phillip's 'the one' and I am more convinced as we spend time together."

She stopped to take a bite of cheesecake before continuing. "We have talked for hours about our lives to this point and, more importantly, what we feel God has for our futures. As we've talked, we both shared our desire to serve God together with our spouse – to be open to that one person God has for us that will not only be our soul mate but will also be a helpmate as we serve the Lord. Speaking just for myself, I believe I have found the man to fit the bill for me. Last but certainly not least, I can say for a surety that I am 100 percent in love with Phillip Doucet and hope that he asks me to marry him soon. If he does, girls, get ready because it won't be a long engagement!"

As Ila talked, Cayden went from surprise to a bit of shock to a firm belief that Ila knew her heart and was open to God's leading in the very important matter of marriage. And, if the look on Allie's face meant anything, she felt the same way. After a long silence, Cayden reached for her friends' hands and took the matter to their Heavenly Father. "Dear Lord, I am blown away by the faith Ila has that you're leading her and Phillip. I'm also sure of her love for this man. Please lead them and direct their paths. Open their hearts to see what you have for them. Thank you for loving us and for wanting us to be happy as we serve you. In Jesus' name, Amen."

"I couldn't have said it better," Allie chimed in through tears. "I teach little people and can read their sincerity and their hearts pretty well. But I've never seen and felt as much clarity and certainty as I've just seen in you, Ila. Just know that I stand ready to help plan a wedding at the drop of a hat, my friend!"

"Me too!" Cayden shouted. "It's going to be such fun watching all this unfold."

Knowing nothing could top that discussion, they finished their dessert and decided to call it a night. Remembering her promise, Cayden did one last thing – pack three large slices of cheesecake to take to the office the next morning. Ila wrote each man's name on one of the containers, which were placed in a bag with a warning sign Allie made. They wanted to make sure no one (Daniel in particular) touched the containers before Wednesday night service. With quick hugs and promises to fervently pray for one another, their girls' night was done and what a night it had been.

# Chapter 12

Cayden got up early Saturday morning to have plenty of time to travel the relatively short, fifty-mile trip to Tysons Corner Center. According to her mapping app, it should only take a little over an hour traveling north on I-95, but traffic could make that a two-hour trip. Luckily, traffic on Saturdays wasn't as heavy as on weekdays; but to be safe, she planned on two hours. After carefully placing a container with a slice of cheesecake and two pumpkin cookies on the passenger floorboard and praying for travelling safety, she turned on her favorite Christmas playlist and set out for a fun day of shopping and catching up with her best friend.

The two girls greeted each other with hugs and tears. Anyone watching, would have thought they hadn't seen one another in six years instead of six months. Marta suggested they find a coffee shop and have a small chat session before doing some serious shopping, which was just what Cayden hoped would happen. Seated at a small table tucked away from holiday shoppers, they chattered away like two magpies for about fifteen minutes before Cayden let out a loud shriek that drew attention from everyone in their vicinity. Unperturbed by this outburst, Marta sat still with the goofiest grin on her face as she stared at a lovely diamond solitaire on her left ring finger.

"I wondered how long it would take you to notice! It's taken all my will power to not shout the news but waiting certainly was worth it. You should have seen your face just before you screamed – priceless!" Marta was beaming as Cayden grabbed her hand to inspect the beautiful engagement ring.

"You didn't mention this when we talked Sunday. How dare you not tell me such an important thing! In fact, I mentioned it and you assured me Wade had not proposed." Cayden wasn't sure whether to be angry at Marta for keeping this a secret or to be thrilled. In the end, thrilled won out and she grabbed her best friend in a bear hug while both girls cried tears of excitement and joy.

"I didn't hold back – Wade only proposed last night. We had gone out to Luchera for dinner and I wondered about him taking me to such a fancy place, but chalked it up to the holidays and the fact I would be moving to Texas soon. We ordered our meals and Wade kept shifting around in his chair like something was wrong, so I asked him if everything was okay. Instead of answering, he popped up out of his seat and knelt in front of me all the while trying to open the ring box." At Marta's description, both girls burst out in joyous laughter. "He had planned to wait until dessert but said he knew he would never be able to eat and carry on a conversation during dinner. I wish you could have seen how sweet and nervous he was. You know Wade, he's always calm and confident but not last night." Marta took a break to drink some tea and Cayden jumped in.

"That's so sweet. You two are perfect for each other. I'm so glad he got up the nerve to ask and that's some rock you've got there. Let me see it again now that I've calmed down. Lovely – both the ring and the bride-to-be!" Tears were flowing again as Cayden offered congratulations.

"Well, according to Wade, he couldn't let me move so far away without making sure we were on the same page concerning our future together. We have a lot to discuss with the first order of business to decide if I'll go ahead and take the job in Texas or call them Monday with a refusal. Please pray that we make the right decision," she asked with all sincerity.

Cayden didn't miss a beat but immediately took Marta's hands, bowed her head, and prayed for the couple to clearly hear what God would want them to do and that He would give them the grace to do it. Jokingly, after saying "Amen," she added, "but please let them decide Marta stays in Virginia."

That bit of news changed the whole mood of their day. Instead of just shopping with Christmas in mind, they went in every shop that had wedding attire or household goods. Marta even tried on a few wedding gowns and veils, which had them crying again but tears of joy mixed with giddiness.

Lunch had been planned as a casual fast-food meal but changed to a nice restaurant where they could sit and discuss wedding plans. Conversation eventually turned to what else was new in their lives. Marta caught Cayden up on all her family and what had been happening with them. As friends do, Cayden reciprocated by filling Marta in on what was new in her world. She updated her on the Ila and Phillip budding relationship and even touched on a possibility of something she'd seen between Allie and Luke Sunday night. She tied it all up nicely with an overview of how God was answering her and her mom's prayers. Her desire to feel useful was being met big time and she was making new, lasting friendships.

They laughed as they recited their favorite praise together, "God is good all the time, and all the time God is good!"

It was after four o'clock that afternoon before they said their goodbyes and the goodies container was transferred to Marta's car. They promised to keep in touch and to make it a point to get together at least one more time before Christmas. There was even talk of Marta and Wade coming to Fredericksburg for a weekend. Marta would stay with Cayden and Wade could maybe bunk with Daniel or book a night at Ellen's Shamrock Inn. With honks of their car horns, one girl headed north and one south. It was going to be a great Christmas season.

On the way home, Cayden mused over her day and the joy she saw in Marta. She sent up a quick prayer for guidance for Marta and Wade as they made important life decisions together. She also prayed for Ila and Phillip and for the Lord to lead in their relationship. It seemed that love was in the air this Christmas and she didn't mind at all that it did not include her just yet.

# Chapter 13

The first week of December was cold with snow flurries but no accumulation. While some people hoped for a white Christmas, Daniel just enjoyed the cold, crisp days with hopes of one last hike up Old Rag Mountain before the year was out. He would have to find someone willing to brave the elements and spend the day enjoying the climb. One thing he was sure of – that person would not be Cayden. While she liked to hike, he had picked up on the fact she did not particularly like cold weather. Maybe in the spring he would invite her to join him on a hike to Dark Hollow Falls off the Skyline Drive. The excursion would take several hours but the falls were worth the effort.

A voice interrupted his daydreaming, and he looked up to find the lady in question standing in his office doorway. Waving her hand in front of his face, she said, "Hey, earth to Daniel. Since it's Friday and we're not busy, Pastor said we could start the weekend early. Just wanted you to know I'm leaving. Everything okay? You were miles away."

"Oh, just thinking about one last mountain hike before we get a serious snow. Wouldn't be interested, would you?" Even though he knew the answer, it was fun watching her expression as the mere thought of a winter hike flitted across her mind.

"It would take a team of horses to pull me screaming and kicking to do such a thing in this cold. But, Mr. Garrett, I think you knew my answer before you asked. Nope, I need to stop by the mall before joining Allie for dinner, after which I plan to curl up on my sofa with a new Sharon Srock book and a big mug of hot cocoa." Turning to leave, she added, "Don't forget Jeff invited our young adult class over for chili and game night tomorrow evening. You planning to join us?" Cayden rattled off her weekend plans as she pulled on gloves and a knit cap – nope, this girl did not like cold, which was funny because she loved snow.

Rising from his desk and grabbing his jacket, Daniel thanked her for the reminder. "Are we supposed to bring anything or just show up hungry?"

"I imagine some of us will bring a dessert but don't worry I'll bring enough to cover your contribution too. How's that?" For the thousandth time, Cayden thought how much Daniel reminded her of her kid brother. Even after working together for six months, she still often marveled to realize Daniel was her senior by six years. But she was surprised to realize that it didn't bother her the way it did when she first arrived. He had a sort of boyish charm instead of an annoying way that Carter often exhibited to his big sister.

After thanking Cayden, he walked with her to their cars, and they parted ways. It had been kind of her to volunteer to do something nice like that. If she had asked what she should bring, he would have quickly shared his fondest hope for cheesecake.

Since Daniel taught Sunday school and was often involved with children's ministries during other services, he sometimes felt out of the loop when it came to the young adults at church. But one thing he was sure of was there would be lots of laughter, food, and fellowship. Jeff and Teresa were great hosts and knew how to make everyone feel welcome, along with always providing a ton of great food.

Arriving early in case Jeff could use a hand setting up, Daniel felt comfortable and at home. Their farmhouse had been the setting for many church activities over the three years he had been at Southside. Plus, he and their son, Luke, had become good friends. He had just finished setting out some folding chairs in the large family room when Luke came in with his girlfriend, Karla. Soon, the house was buzzing with happy voices and friendly smack talk about some new game they would be playing.

Allie had come in with Ila and Phillip but still no sign of Cayden and the promised dessert. Daniel was surprised to find himself beginning to worry – where had that come from? Well, he supposed, it was only kind to be concerned for a young lady on her own in a relatively new city. With that settled, he joined in a conversation about football but kept an eye on the door. After all, she was bringing dessert.

A few minutes later, Cayden arrived followed by a tall guy he was sure wasn't part of the young adult group, at least not that he'd ever seen. Moving closer, he heard Cayden's introduction of her guest. "Everyone, this is my friend Josh Linden, who is visiting from Georgia. We went to Liberty together." While the guy was smiling, Daniel noticed something cross his face as she finished the introduction, like he had expected her to elaborate more. Daniel made a mental note to investigate further – if not tonight, then Monday at work. Again, he wondered where these thoughts were coming from but brushed them away. Girls had always intrigued but confused him and Cayden was no exception. But one good thing – she had brought cheesecake!

The night soon progressed from a devotion time to chili with all the fixings and on to games. Even with more than twenty adults, there was plenty of room for everyone to join in a game of their choice or even have some quiet catch-up time with friends. While most of the guests were unmarried, there were a few married couples who had been blessed with children and who were happy to just relax and enjoy some much-needed time with people their own age.

Daniel noticed that Phillip and Ila's relationship had bloomed until now it was evident to anyone with eyes that they were an actual "couple." One was never far from the other and he even saw them holding hands as they moved through the evening. Knowing they were both praying for God's direction in their lives, he stepped out onto the front porch and lifted them up to the Father for guidance in making a lifetime commitment to each other. As if on cue, Phillip joined him in the quiet of the night.

"Hey, Jeff wants you to lead in some singing. So, I volunteered to find you. Everything okay? It's not like you to not be in the middle of everything," Phillip asked as he rubbed his hands for warmth.

"As a matter of fact, I was praying for you and Ila. Since the night we had coffee with the girls, you've gotten a lot closer. Is that a sign you two might be heading into a serious relationship – you know, like marriage?" Daniel laughed as he watched the expressions flit across Phillip's face. He had never thought about it but a man in love could be quite comical.

"We have discussed it and are both praying for God to make His will abundantly clear to us. But I've got to tell you that even though it's only been a month since we met, I'm crazy about her. If God asked me to describe the perfect woman for me, Ila would be the model. And, truthfully, I'm pretty sure she feels the same way, but we've agreed to take the time to be sure. Plus, this dating thing is fun! Thank you for praying – that means a lot. Now, we better get back in there before they send a search party." Phillip ushered Daniel back into the house. Phillip found Ila, while Daniel's eyes easily landed on Cayden.

The highlight of the evening came when the group divided into two teams for Pictionary. Drawing skills ranged from non-existent to rather talented, which added to the fun, along with the competitive nature sprinkled throughout the teams. Daniel thought that he was beginning to know Cayden pretty well but realized there was one aspect of her personality he had not experienced until that game – the girl was competitive. As captain of their team, she quickly evolved from pleasant, easygoing Cayden to what he would henceforth refer to as "Killer Cayden." Stories would later be told (with some embellishment) how that at one point during the game, he almost had to restrain her physically from assaulting Phillip, who it turned out was equally competitive. Luckily, there was no bloodshed and the night ended on a happy note.

To say the least, Cayden had been surprised when Josh called Saturday morning. They dated for a few months the summer following her junior year. By the time school reconvened, she realized they might be better suited as friends. She sometimes saw him around campus but they didn't speak again. So, seeing his name flash on her cell phone screen was a bit shocking.

Since graduation, he had landed a job as a Communications Specialist for a power company in the Athens area. He had grown up in a small town just south of Athens and enjoyed living close to family again. Since he was in the Northern Virginia area for a week to attend a training conference, he decided to try to touch base with Cayden and maybe meet up for dinner. She wondered how he knew where she lived until he mentioned looking her up on Facebook, where she had happily updated her information to include her new job in Fredericksburg. His invitation to have dinner together wound up with them at Jeff and Teresa's for chili and game night, which was a good way for them to start getting reacquainted.

When Josh took Cayden home and asked if he could come up, she was shocked to find it was almost eleven o'clock. Realizing she was enjoying time with him more than expected, she agreed with a smile. "Okay, but just for a one cup of coffee. I need to go over my Sunday school lesson one more time tonight. I'm teaching Renee's class again and those seven-year-olds keep me on my toes."

A look crossed his face but was quickly replaced with a grin as he agreed to just a cup of coffee if she promised to have dinner with him on Sunday after church. Happiness spread through her as she thought of spending more time with this seemingly new, more mature Josh. A quick agreement was reached, and they raced up the stairs to get out of the cold drizzle that had just begun. True to his word, after one cup, he kissed her cheek and left, promising to make it in time for worship service the next morning.

Cayden dressed for bed and did a final review of tomorrow's lesson. This time she would be teaching them about Gideon and how he put a fleece out on two occasions asking God to show him what he was to do. In both instances, God answered Gideon's request, giving him clear direction on the path he should take.

After a deep breath, she prayed, "Father, you've brought Josh back into my life for a reason. I'm not sure what that might be, but I trust you to know the direction you have for my life in this particular area. So, please show me if a romantic relationship with Josh is what you have for me or not. Thank you, Lord. Amen." After turning it over to the Lord, she quickly fell asleep and awoke the next morning ready to see how His plan unfolded. Sometimes, it was just plain amazing to watch His hand move in her life.

Daniel was surprised when he came to the podium Sunday morning to open the service and saw Josh in the congregation. From conversation the night before, he didn't get the feeling there was a lot going on between Josh and Cayden. But then maybe he hadn't read the situation correctly. The guy seemed nice enough but not really Cayden's type, which made him wonder what was her type? And why did it matter? He knew he needed to mind his own business, but it felt like some of the joy had slipped from his day. Not wanting to look too closely at that thought, he jumped enthusiastically into the song service.

Worshipping with Josh was nice. He knew the hymns and sang along seeming to enjoy the service. Afterwards, Cayden introduced him to Pastor Harwell and a few of the others in their general vicinity. Soon, they were seated at her favorite Mexican restaurant. When the waitress called her by name and asked if she wanted her usual, Josh correctly deduced that since the restaurant was almost next door to the church it must be her favorite lunch spot.

"Well, that's something that hasn't changed. When we were dating, you almost always wanted Mexican and not just from any old spot. It had to be the café closest to campus. I hope they were able to keep the doors open after you and Marta graduated." Even though Josh was joking, it was true. That restaurant had been their place to celebrate, collaborate, or commiserate and their food was the most authentic according to Marta.

"When your roommate's mother cooks the real stuff and she's even willing to take her mother there to eat, you know it's got to be good," Cayden quickly informed him.

They hadn't had much time to talk the night before and found conversation a bit stiff at first. But by the time the first basket of warm tortilla chips with salsa was consumed, they found it easier to relax as they caught up on over a year's worth of living. She told him all about how God's hand was evident in leading her to Fredericksburg and her job. He listened intently but didn't seem overly impressed with the obvious signs of God working in her life. Before she had time to think it over, the waitress brought the check, and they were soon exiting the restaurant with warm goodbyes from the wait staff.

Taking her hand as they walked to the car, he asked, "Is there a place we could take a walk? I'll be sitting in classes for the next four days and could use the exercise."

Even though it was December, the temperature was at least above freezing. Although it was a bit too cold for a walk, Cayden reasoned that the exercise would soon warm her up. Agreeing that was a good idea, she directed him to the Heritage Trail that ran alongside the Rappahannock River. It was paved and the river views were lovely.

As they walked, he again took her hand before sharing more about his job and his plans for one day being CEO. At first, she thought he was joking considering the fact he had just graduated college and was only a few months into his first job but one glance at his face confirmed he was quite serious.

"It's a small electric company and there are obvious career opportunities. Most of the senior staff will be retirement age over the next ten years, which means I need to take every opportunity to make myself shine to advance quickly. In fact, I've decided to begin work on my master's degree. Isn't that exciting?" His eyes sparkled as he talked, and it was obvious he was over the moon with his plans.

"Wow, that's wonderful! You have it all planned out and I hope it works just as you see it. Are you praying about which program you should choose?" she asked.

"Oh, that's easy. I've talked with my boss to see which school she thinks would be best. In fact, last week I invited her boss to lunch to discuss furthering my career in the company. He seemed impressed I would be planning ahead." Josh was almost glowing as he outlined his plans and how he thought was the best way to achieve them.

"Yes, but all through school we were taught to seek God's will especially in the big decisions and I'm sure your parents taught you that at home," Cayden gently reminded him.

He seemed to be deciding how best to answer. "You know I only went to a Christian college to appease my folks. While I believe in God, I'm not as enthusiastic as you are, always having to include Him in every aspect of my life. He gave me a brain and expects me to use it, which is what I'm doing. No offense, I just don't feel the way you do."

"Have you found a church in Athens or are you going to your home church in Watkinsville with your parents?" Cayden asked. "Because you know as well as I do that a good church is an important part of growing in the Lord. You can't expect to just run to God when you need something and forget about Him the rest of the time. Going your own way may seem the right thing to do but it's not the best thing and I want the best for you."

Dropping her hand and putting his hand in his pocket, Josh picked up the pace as they approached his car. "You have your beliefs and I have mine. Believing that God is looking at your little life and making your car break down just so that you wind up being a secretary in a church seems a bit childlike. Your parents spent a lot of money on your education and you're throwing it away on a dead-end job with no prospects. How can you say that's God's best for you?"

As she got in the car, Cayden took a deep breath before responding. "All my parents want for me is the best out of life and that means finding God's will for me and following it. They are thrilled about the path God has me on because they can see it as plainly as I do. When you pray earnestly for God to lead you where He wants you to go in life and He shows it to you, that's what makes life worth living. I still marvel every day that the God who created the universe loves me enough to care about my life and I want to live it to His glory."

The trip back to church was quiet. He broke the silence as he parked beside her car. "I appreciate your viewpoint but it's not mine. I will get to where I want to be by being tenacious, observant, and conscientious. And to answer your earlier question, no, I haven't attended church since leaving school."

"Oh!" was all Cayden could think to say at first but then quickly added one last thing before getting into her car. "You probably won't appreciate this, but I will be praying for you that your eyes are opened to the power that's found only in following God's will for your life. Thank you for looking me up and taking me to dinner today. It was nice catching up. Please give your parents my best regards."

As he closed her car door, Josh looked uncomfortable not knowing how to respond. So, he just bid her farewell and before she even had her car in drive, he was already speeding out of the parking lot.

She sat still waiting for her emotions to settle. Josh had never exhibited this type of distaste for church or for God while they were dating. Thinking back to those few months, she realized she hadn't done a lot of praying about dating him. She'd sort of thought anyone at a Christian school would believe in God but that was naïve thinking, and she could see that now. Taking another moment, she bowed her head and thanked the Lord for once again showing her clearly what path to take. She would pray for Josh but that was the end of that.

Try as she might, when she laid down that night, sleep eluded her because her mind kept drifting back over the last two days. More than she had realized, her hopes had gotten up thinking maybe romance was in the making for her and Josh – or her and anyone. That surprised her and also made her a bit sad. Her mind turned to advice that her mom had given her a long time ago that basically said she wasn't supposed to look for happiness in another person. It wasn't fair or wise to put that burden on someone. True happiness had to come within herself, and it needed to be rooted in her relationship with God and being willing to wait for His direction and timing. As she thought this over, she took her cares to the Lord again asking for His direction in her life, including if or when romance was to be a part of her future. She fell into a peaceful sleep quoting her now favorite verse, Jeremiah 29:11.

# Chapter 14

C ayden was in for a surprise Monday morning when she opened the blinds to find at least two inches of snow on the ground and more falling in big, fluffy flakes. She didn't have a lot of experience driving in snow while growing up in Virginia Beach but had learned a little more during her four years in Lynchburg.

While she might not like cold weather, she loved snow and was almost giddy with anticipation to see what transpired as she dressed warmly for her trek into work. Stopping for a minute, she sent up thanks that Beth and Don had insisted on arranging their garage so she could park inside. Both of their vehicles were safely parked in the garage attached to their house, which only left Don's red 1965 Pontiac GTO convertible in the detached garage.

A sound she couldn't instantly identify came from outside her door. When she checked it out, she found Don sweeping snow from her stairway and landing. Opening the door, she invited him in for coffee. Stepping inside after brushing snow from his overalls and hair, he accepted the proffered cup with a sigh.

"Thanks, Cayden! I'll just stand here on the rug and enjoy the warmth. Boy, did the weatherman miss it when he predicted only flurries today." Taking a quick sip, he continued, "Will you be okay to drive in this or would you like me to take you to work? I feel pretty sure the roads should be plowed and salted but it can still be slick in places."

"Oh, with the CR-V having all-wheel drive, I should be fine. I'm excited to get out in the snow!" she finished with a grin. But seeing the look on his face, she toned it down a bit and promised to take care.

Just then they heard a car pull into the driveway, quickly followed by footsteps on the stairs to her apartment. Before Daniel could knock, Don pulled the door open and motioned him in. Cayden stood nearby welcoming him all the while wondering what he was doing there.

"Hi guys. I thought Cayden might want to ride into work with me since they're now calling for up to six inches of this stuff." His greeting was received with looks of surprise from both Don and Cayden, as this seemed a bit out of the norm for Daniel. But Don quickly agreed that sounded like a good idea since Daniel's Jeep would do great in snow. Accepting that six inches of snow might be a bit more than she would be comfortable navigating, Cayden couldn't think of a reason to decline.

"That would be very nice, Daniel. Thanks for thinking of me! I'll be ready in just a minute. Grab a cup of coffee if you want to while I finish getting ready. Just pop in a k-cup and choose the strength." She continued giving instructions as she walked to her bedroom, "Mugs are in the cabinet directly overhead."

Don finished his coffee, said goodbye and left to sweep the stairs one last time before heading back home. Daniel brewed his coffee and stood near the door for the few minutes it took for Cayden to reappear in her coat, boots, gloves, and knit cap. Draining his cup, he rinsed it out before putting it in the dishwasher.

Cayden noticed and remarked, "Your Mama trained you well. Thanks for doing that! I like to leave the apartment neat but especially the kitchen. Now, let's get out in the snow!"

A bit taken aback, Daniel responded as they traipsed to his Jeep, "But you hate cold. How can you be so excited about snow?"

"When you grow up where a lot of snow isn't usual, you get excited. Seriously, though, I appreciate your thoughtfulness to offer me a ride. I think it put Don's mind at ease as well as saved me all the trouble of cleaning off my vehicle later today," Cayden responded while getting situated in the Jeep. This was going to be a fun day.

The usual ten-minute trip to work was doubled due to slower driving and having to navigate around a small fender-bender. Not long into the ride, Cayden realized this was really the longest time they had spent alone together other than a few meals in restaurants and their kayaking trip. At work, he was in his office and their time talking was most often as he passed through on his way out, stopping for a quick chat.

Cayden asked about his weekend, and he asked about hers before they settled into discussing the great time everyone had at Jeff and Teresa's Saturday night. As she feared, he referred to her as "Killer Cayden" a few times and she knew the nickname was going to stick.

Daniel asked if Josh enjoyed his visit. "I hadn't realized you were bringing a guest. Were you in a lot of the same classes or did you go to church together on campus? He seemed a bit put off when you introduced him as a friend from school. Seemed like he expected a bit more of an introduction."

Not thinking of Daniel as very perceptive, Cayden was surprised he had seen the look Josh had given her. "We did have one or two classes together junior year and dated for a few months but called it quits before we started our senior year. Frankly, his calling came as a shock, but it was nice to catch up with what's going on in his life."

"Sounded like he would be here for most of the week. Will we be seeing him again this trip?" he asked innocently.

Searching for the right words, Cayden looked out the window before giving Daniel a brief sketch of their Sunday afternoon conversation. "So, no, we won't be seeing Josh again this trip or the next one either."

Just as she finished speaking, he pulled up under the portico at the doorway leading to their offices. The snow under the portico wasn't very deep but Daniel insisted he walk with her into the building before parking. He quickly dismissed her thanks explaining that she couldn't fall and break a leg on his watch, or he would never live it down. Thus, the status quo was re-established of office buddies and nothing more (or was there?).

Shortly before noon, Pastor Harwell called advising them to head home. Apparently, the snow was going to continue into the night. He also told them to plan on working from home the next day. As soon as Daniel finished talking with Pastor, Beth called inviting them to lunch. She had made a huge pot of soup, had the makings for grilled cheese sandwiches, and brownies were in the oven. Cayden had switched to speakerphone so Daniel could hear the invitation and he was almost shouting "Yes!" before Beth finished talking. Following was a flurry of gathering laptops and files before getting into their coats and other winter attire. Just like kids being released from school, Cayden and Daniel were almost giddy with excitement.

Lunch was the perfect snowy day meal – hot, filling, and delicious. An unexpected plus was Don joining them. It seemed everyone was canceling appointments and those not canceled were quickly rescheduled to later in the week when the temperatures were forecasted to be in the mid-forties.

Talk centered around what was going on around the church and Saturday night's young adult Christmas party. Of course, Daniel regaled them with his rendition of the "Killer Cayden" Pictionary game, to which she added how much everyone loved it when Daniel looked at the wrong word to draw and was trying to get his team to guess something totally different than the other team. Conversation drifted to upcoming teen activities and eventually landed on Josh. Cayden gave them the same brief description of his visit before quickly turning the conversation to their neighbors Paula and Mrs. Virginia.

"I've been meaning to drop by and see how they're doing but time gets away from me. I think I'll go over there this afternoon and visit for a few minutes. They might need something from the store, and I could go for them." As she talked, the idea grew to a certainty that she should do just that – make sure they were doing okay.

Daniel offered to take her over since he had begun praying for them after Cayden told him about Mrs. Virginia falling. Beth was soon dishing soup into a container and putting brownies in a storage bag. Daniel even asked Don to borrow a shovel in case their sidewalk needed shoveling. Thinking that a grand idea, Don volunteered to join them.

"Well, if you all are going, I'm going too," Beth said from the kitchen. "I'll just need a minute to get ready." And, just like that, their party of four went calling hoping to be a blessing to the ladies next door.

Paula was at the door by the time they tramped through the snow to her side door. The look on her face wasn't necessarily friendly but it wasn't unfriendly and that was encouraging. She invited them in and offered tea or coffee after they removed their coats and boots. Appreciating the hospitality, they settled in for a visit as Paula served hot drinks. Paula's eyes lit up when Beth handed her the box with soup and sweets, and she quickly put brownies on saucers for everyone.

Cayden took a sip of tea before asking, "How is Mrs. Virginia? Is she asleep?"

Sitting down at the table with her coffee, Paula advised them that her mother was taking a nap and was doing quite well physically with no aftereffects of the fall.

Noticing how tired Paula was looking, Beth asked if her mother was doing better sleeping at night. Unfortunately, Paula's answer was a rather sad

"No. If anything, she's a little worse in that department and I can't get much rest with her up and down all night. I'm going to downsize the animals on the farm, which will be one burden removed. It makes my heart hurt but it's either that or I may not be able to keep on looking after mother. Chores on a farm can't be put on hold just because I'm too tired to do them. But I'm happy to have mother here with me and she's my chief concern." Shaking her head, she added a request to let her know if they heard of anyone who might be in the market for some horses, a cow or a few chickens.

Daniel was the first to respond. "One of the guys at church just bought a small farm outside Stafford and I heard him mention adding some animals. I'll text him if you like and then call you with his contact information." A plan was put into place and before they were ready to leave, he was jotting down Paula's phone number and assuring her his friend was a reliable, trustworthy man. He seemed to sense that she wouldn't want just anyone having her farm "babies."

Shortly after finishing their coffee, Don and Daniel set out to shovel paths for Paula and to clean off her vehicle. They were even able to rearrange some things in her garage so that she could drive her Bronco in out of the weather.

The ladies were enjoying their comfortable conversation when Paula heard her mother stirring via a baby monitor. The look on her face indicated she would prefer they leave as opposed to having Mrs. Virginia join them. "Mother isn't at her best after waking or I would ask you to stay and visit with her."

Glancing at her watch, Cayden apologized, "I'm so sorry. We only meant to visit for a few minutes and look at the time. We've got to get moving. Would it be okay if we came back to check on you tomorrow and maybe visit with Mrs. Virginia?"

Paula seemed to brighten at the thought of another visit. So, after making sure she needed nothing from the store, the ladies joined the men who had finished shoveling and the group left feeling better for the visit.

Thanks to the snow, three o'clock seemed more like five o'clock as they came back into Beth's kitchen. She quickly declared the only thing to do was to play a game or two and everyone agreed, even Don who wasn't always keen on games.

"Hey, Cayden, I've been meaning to discuss something with you as your landlord," Don said with an expression she couldn't read. Seeing the worried look on Cayden's face, he quickly followed this up with, "I saw how you reacted when Renee mentioned she had some puppies needing homes. Our niece, Melissa, had a dog when she lived in the apartment and we're okay if you would like to have one. You keep the place immaculate, and we know you would be a responsible pet owner. Sorry to give you a scare about the 'landlord' reference." But his grin belied his innocence. Over the six months since Cayden had moved into the apartment, he and Beth had come to love her and to enjoy her company and Don loved to tease her.

Cayden gave the thought of having a puppy a brief examination before thanking them for their kindness. If the opportunity arose again, she might check out the possibility of having a pet. But she wouldn't go out looking for one.

Realizing it was close to suppertime, Daniel rose to leave only to be invited to stay and eat with them. Beth had popped lasagna in the oven when they got back from Paula's and the aroma pervaded the den where they had been playing Trivial Pursuit. Not one to turn down a home-cooked meal, Daniel accepted and asked how he could help. Before Beth could respond, Don drafted him to help with some shoveling because the snow was still steadily falling.

Dinner was wonderful with good food and a comfortable atmosphere full of laughter and joking. As soon as they'd eaten, Daniel thanked them for a lovely day and left for home. Soon after, kitchen clean, Cayden gave them hugs and heartfelt thanks before traveling the small distance to her apartment home. Throwing a snowball into the air, she thought that maybe tomorrow she'd build a snowman.

The following day, Daniel called to let Cayden know his friend, Jake Abernathy, would be meeting with Paula about her animals that morning. Later, when she arrived at Paula's with freshly baked muffins, Mr. Abernathy had arrived, and Paula was trying to figure out how to show him the farm without leaving her mother alone. Cayden quickly agreed to visit with Mrs. Virginia, who was already commenting on how good the muffins smelled.

When Mr. Abernathy and Paula returned to the warm kitchen, they sat down over coffee and muffins to come up with a plan for the farm animals while Cayden played Uno with Mrs. Virginia. After striking a deal for him to buy all her stock, Mr. Abernathy excused himself with the promise to return the next day to begin moving the animals to his farm. Cayden was glad he had obviously realized the need for Paula to part with her animals but also the need for her to have a chance to tell them goodbye.

By the end of the week, most of the snow had melted and life began gearing up for Christmas in earnest. The choir had been working for weeks practicing for the Christmas cantata and those involved with the live nativity were busy getting all their props and costumes pulled together. Cayden had her hand in much of the preparations for what was happening at church, but her favorite part had been the ladies' Christmas dinner, which was hosted by the men of the church. Deviating from the usual holiday fare, they had chosen instead to go with pasta with marinara or alfredo sauce, salad, rolls, and cheesecake.

Daniel had somehow been wrangled into taking care of the menu and when cheesecake was the dessert choice he came knocking on Cayden's door. Using reasoning that hers was the very best, he quickly had her promise to bake six cheesecakes but only if he helped her. With the use of her oven and Beth's double ovens, they were able to bake all six Friday before the Saturday dinner. Pastor was kind enough to give them the day off since he was promised a piece of the much-coveted delicacy.

That evening, after Daniel left and she was finally alone with her feet up, Cayden realized how much fun she'd had with him. He really could be a cool, funny guy and she found herself wondering about the man she saw almost every day but knew very little about. Filing that thought away for another day, she decided it was bedtime. It had been a good day.

Daniel's reflections ran along the same track as Cayden's except he was beginning to realize the direction his thoughts were taking where she was concerned. Looking back over the months since he'd bought her a Peppermint Patty, he could see signs of a shift in how he thought of the kind, generous, beautiful, godly woman he was blessed to know. Never having fallen in love before, he wasn't sure what was going on, but he knew he needed time to discuss it with God and then with his oldest sister, who knew him better than he knew himself sometimes. He fell asleep on his couch praying that God would direct him.

Cayden was happy how well all the Christmas activities had gone off without too much drama. One child had gotten a bit too close to a donkey in the live nativity and received a tiny nip but with no real damage. The choir cantata was lovely in the candlelit sanctuary even though Daniel had to fill in for one of the soloists at the last minute. Cards and gifts were exchanged with much love and joy as the birth of Jesus was celebrated.

Most of their little group would be spending Christmas with their families. Phillip and Ila's plans included Christmas Eve and Christmas morning at Ila's parents before traveling Christmas afternoon to his parents' home in Raleigh. The group, along with Luke, had gone out after church Wednesday night to Olaf's but this time the girls paid for coffee. Cayden presented each guy with a hand-made coupon for one cheesecake with the proviso that the baker must be given a two-day notice. She, Allie, and Ila had exchanged gifts the night before at their weekly girls' night dinner.

The Friday before Christmas was their last day in the office and was exceptionally fun. Knowing birthdays during the holiday season could be downplayed and sometimes overlooked, Cayden planned a surprise party for lunchtime to celebrate Daniel's Christmas Eve birthday. His mom and dad along with the teens were invited to the Mexican themed party. Parents brought in Mexican dishes and there was even a pinata for part of the entertainment. Renee made a cake that looked like a huge taco and adorned it with magic relighting candles. The teens really enjoyed watching Pastor Daniel trying to blow them out to no avail.

Christmas fell on a Monday and the church office was going to be closed for the entire Christmas week. Pastor was staying in town for the holidays and would take lead on any need that arose while Daniel and Cayden were "on call" if needed. After all, the needs of the congregation did not take a holiday.

Cayden left for Virginia Beach after Christmas Eve service Sunday morning. She and a lot of others were traveling south for the holiday but this time she knew some back roads that helped when traffic began to back up. Being with her family for a week was worth the travel woes.

# Chapter 15

As wonderful as Christmas at home had been, Cayden found herself happy to be back in her own home late Thursday afternoon. Traffic hadn't been crazy, and she was looking forward to catching up with her friends and to soon welcoming a new year. After everything that had transpired in her life over the last twelve months, she was anxious to see what the new year would hold. She felt comfortable in her life, and she thanked God every day for leading her.

Friday morning, after a run and a shower, she busied herself putting away Christmas gifts, which meant rearranging some cabinets and drawers. A quick trip to the mall to exchange a couple of things and she was ready for girls' night dinner at Allie's.

Gathered around a table in the quaint Italian restaurant near Allie's farm, the three girls talked non-stop except to eat. Allie shared news from church, which was followed with the usual Christmas conversation about family, friends, and gifts received. Not until they were comfortably seated in front of the large fireplace in Allie's sitting room did the real catch-up begin.

Excited to hear what had been happening in her absence, Cayden declared that as hostess, Allie should start them off. Taking a deep breath, Allie filled them in on some news she was sure they would enjoy.

"Actually, I do have news to report. Joey and Gil took me skiing Tuesday. We spent the day at Wintergreen and the slopes were great." She finished with a smile as if that was the end of the story but the pink in her cheeks told Ila there was more to learn about their skiing trip.

"That's where Phillip and Daniel are going tomorrow with your brothers, and I think even Luke is going to join them. But I think you haven't finished telling us everything. What haven't you told us? You might as well spill it all because you know we'll find out one way or another." Ila knew one call to Allie's oldest brother, Gil, and she would at least have enough of a clue to start digging.

"Okay, okay, there's a bit more if you really must know." Allie was suddenly grinning and telling them everything. "Let's just say that Tuesday was a great example of why having older brothers can come in handy. They introduced me to one of the ski instructors, Rod Parlett, and we're having dinner tomorrow night!"

Cayden was so excited she almost spilled her cocoa. "No way! You sat through an entire dinner with your best friends and didn't say a word. Now, tell us about this ski instructor!"

Happy to oblige, Allie gave them the details of what had turned out to be a fun day. Although her brothers weren't easy to obtain information from, she was able to ascertain that Rod was single, a Christian, and an all-around good guy. His classes lasted most of the day but he had joined them after dinner for night skiing. As they skied, he paired up with Allie, which gave them a little time to chat. Afterwards, he treated them to coffee in the staff lounge. While her brothers were busy packing up gear, Rod asked if she would like to have dinner with him.

"And that's about it except for the flowers that arrived Wednesday and the daily calls," she finished up with a dreamy look on her face. Pillows were thrown at her as shrieks of laughter filled the room. "I'm trying not to get too excited, but he sure is nice, and you are going to love him."

After a fun-filled question and answer session, eyes turned to Cayden for an update on what had been happening in her life. "I don't really have anything to report. After the Josh debacle, nothing even remotely resembling romance has happened."

Ila was first to speak up. "We never did get a chance to discuss how that situation affected you. We only got the details of conversations, but it must not have been easy to have him come back into your life and then be gone again just like that." She finished with a click of her fingers.

Cayden took a minute before replying, "Well, my mind has not, and I repeat not, been on romance. But I'll admit that when Josh reappeared, I thought maybe God had other ideas for me. I went to bed Saturday night praying for God to show me where He was leading and if it, indeed, would include Josh. On Sunday when Josh so clearly let me see how he doesn't see the need for God in his life, I had my answer. Yes, it stung a bit and I cried for all of two minutes before realizing I'd dodged a bullet and seeing reason to praise God for His watchcare over me."

"Allie and I talked that Sunday morning and found that we both were praying for God's guidance and His hand of protection over you." Ila reached over to give Cayden a side hug before continuing. "And we're still praying that for you. God has someone special for you, Cayden my girl, just you wait and see!"

Trying to keep them from getting too maudlin, Cayden turned the conversation to Ila and her Christmas excursion to North Carolina. "So, now we come to the main event, Ila Bennett, spill the beans! Tell us everything about your Christmas and Phillip's family. Do you still think he's 'the one'?"

Ila didn't miss a beat before telling her best friends in the entire world how wonderful her visit had been. "Of course, I had to be careful not to just blurt out to Mrs. Doucet that I plan to marry her son! But all joking aside, I truly believe that visit answered any remaining questions we might have had about each other. During the trip back home, we talked about the future in a more concrete way than ever before. The new year is already starting to fill up with invitations for Phillip to speak about *Feed My Sheep* and not only on the east coast. The next couple of months will be interesting because he will be gone more, and we'll see how we handle that. We're both still praying, along with just about everyone else in our lives." As the others nodded agreement, she finished with a reminder. "Keep praying, girls, and be ready to eat lots of ice cream with me when he's traveling and we can't see each other."

Everyone agreed all that was left to do on this wonderful night full of laughter and sharing was to talk to their Heavenly Father. After a time of prayer, Cayden and Ila gave Allie hugs before heading to their homes. Allie stood for a few minutes in the crisp December night wondering just what the Father had in store for the three of them in the coming new year. One thing for sure – it was going to be interesting!

Don and Beth hosted a party after church on New Year's Eve inviting most of the Sunday night church crowd over for food and fellowship to usher in 2018. Cayden took on the duty of welcoming everyone and taking their coats. She was happily surprised when she opened the door to find Paula looking as if she might turn and run back home, which prompted Cayden to give her a hug as she led her into the foyer.

"Paula, you came, how wonderful! Where's Mrs. Virginia?" She talked as she continued to walk Paula further into the house.

Paula gave a tentative smile before answering. "My niece is home from college, and she volunteered to stay with mom tonight. I made sure she had eaten dinner and was already settled in bed before I came over. Must admit though – it's odd to be out without having to worry about mom."

"You have your cell, right? If your niece runs into any problems or has a question, we'll have you home in three minutes tops," Cayden reminded her. "Let me take you upstairs where it's warmer and all the fun's happening. Just two hours until we enter the new year!"

After safely turning Paula over to Beth, Cayden returned to her duties for another fifteen minutes before reckoning anyone who planned to attend would have arrived. Joining the others, she filled the remaining hours of a most unusual year with new friends, who in just six months meant the world to her. She was ready for the new year and the adventures God had in store for her.

As Cayden and Beth walked into worship service the following Sunday morning, they had a wonderful surprise when they spotted Paula sitting on the back pew looking a bit like she was contemplating a quick exit. They welcomed her with hugs and big smiles.

She took a deep breath and admitted, "I was scared half to death to come but meeting some of your friends at the party made me a little curious about your church. My idea of church isn't like what you all describe."

Beth chuckled and waved her hand at the people in the auditorium, "You mean all this hubbub and chatter?"

"Actually, yes," Paula conceded. "The few times I've attended a church service it was very staid and ceremonial. There wasn't a friendly, happy feeling and there definitely wasn't a lot of laughter."

Cayden piped in, "We're just glad you joined us. If you don't mind, I'll sit with you."

That seemed to put Paula at ease as she scooted over to make room. She then answered the question that Cayden was about to ask. "My niece is still in town and offered to stay with mom today to give me a break. At first, I wasn't sure what to do with time on my hands until I recalled your invitation to visit any time and here I am. I hope that's okay."

"Okay? It's more than okay," Beth assured her. "In fact, we insist you join us for lunch after the service. Cayden, Ellen, Don and I are going to Angelica's for some good home cooking, and you just have to come with us." And with that she was off to find Ellen.

Cayden could see the indecision on Paula's face and quickly seconded the invitation, along with reassuring her that it would make them all happy. At about that same time, Daniel walked by but quickly stopped when he saw who Cayden was talking to. By the time church started, their lunch group had grown to include Daniel, Allie, and Ila.

Unknown to Paula, all throughout the service, silent prayers were going up on her behalf. Prayers that she would feel the calm and love of the Holy Spirit and that she would listen to the message of salvation clearly presented during Pastor's sermon. Cayden tried not to look at Paula but couldn't help taking sideways glances just to gage her reaction to what she was hearing. The look on Paula's face was one of interest and something akin to awe as she learned that God loved her and that Jesus had died to pay the debt for her sins. Cayden's prayer turned to a prayer of thanks that her friend was hearing about a Savior who would change her life if she just let Him.

Lunch was a fun time for Paula and this group of new friends she found so intriguing. They really didn't know her and had only just begun to be a part of her life but yet she believed they actually cared about her and her mother. As she watched them interact with each other and include her in their group of friends, she determined to understand what made them different. She also determined to learn more about Jesus and why He would love her. So many new ideas were running through her mind as she drove back home and one thing she knew – she would be going back to that church next Sunday to find answers.

The third week of January found the temperatures hovering in the low fifties and the sun shone most days. Cayden jogged some mornings before work and hurried home to break out her bike for a quick ride before dark several afternoons. Saturday morning was the highlight of the week with the warmest day yet. She got up, stretched, ate a light breakfast, and took off for a nice, long ride. Her neighborhood and the surrounding area were a great place to bike with decent roadways and without a lot of traffic.

After several miles, she stopped for a break before starting the trip back home. As she was putting her water bottle back in her pack, she heard something like a whimper. Sitting very still and quiet, she listened to determine what she'd heard. Not hearing anything, she began slowly pedaling toward her apartment. She hadn't gone very far before a small black and white creature darted out in front of her. Coming to a quick stop, she looked around all the while hoping it wasn't a skunk she had seen. But out of the corner of her eye, she saw a small black dog with a white belly staring at her from the weeds alongside the road. Looking around, she realized there were no houses in the immediate vicinity. She mulled it over and realized she couldn't just leave the puppy where it might run out into traffic or where a larger animal might harm it.

Quietly Cayden called to the pup, "Here, boy. Come on." Slowly the little black and white ball of fur came out of the weeds running toward her. In fact, he ran so fast his little legs got tangled and he went flying head over heels. Holding out her hand for him to sniff, she quickly looked for a collar with tags but found none. "Come on, boy. Let's have a look at you," she crooned as she reached out to pick him up. Thinking he might run away, she was ready to grab him but that wasn't necessary because the little fella jumped up into her hands mewing and licking her fingers.

Her inspection found that he looked to be in good health with no obvious injuries. He seemed a little skinny underneath all his fur, which was another indicator he might not have a home. Thinking of what she had in her pack, she took out some crackers and offered one to him and he gladly gobbled it up. Three crackers later, he curled up in her hands seemingly ready for a nap. No mistaking it, she had a new buddy. Now, she had to figure out her next step.

Carter had teased her when she had outfitted her bike with a basket but now, she was glad she had somewhere to put the sleeping puppy. She placed her jacket in the basket and laid him on it before starting off for home. As she rode along, she took notice of the location and houses so she could come back asking if anyone knew to whom he belonged. For the moment, she felt he needed proper nourishment and to be checked for things like fleas, ticks, and other puppy maladies. She was properly having her first adventure of the new year and was wondering where it would lead.

Organizing her thoughts on what had to be done and in what order wasn't easy as she peeked at the cute little ball of fur. Don and Beth were in Tennessee visiting relatives and calling her parents wouldn't be much help since they were over two hours away. Suddenly, she had the answer – Ila! She always knew what to do, but a quick call went straight to voicemail. Calling

Allie was next but as she arrived home, she saw Daniel's Jeep in the driveway and Daniel sitting on the steps to her apartment. Animals weren't something they had ever discussed but maybe he could help.

Before she came to a complete stop, he was walking toward her and gazing at the puppy who was just waking up. "What have you got there? I didn't know you had a puppy!"

"I don't, at least I don't think I do. He was alongside the road in an area with no houses and I couldn't leave him there," she poured out in one big breath. "You don't by chance know of any vets in the area who might be open on a Saturday afternoon, do you?"

Mulling it over while petting the puppy, Daniel pulled out his phone and dialed a number. "This might get us in to see a vet today or maybe tomorrow sometime." Someone answered the call, and he quickly explained the situation to them. After answering a few questions, he hung up with a smile. "My friend, Mia, works in an emergency vet office and she can squeeze us in if we go right now. Does that work?"

"Are you joking? Just like that, we can see a vet? Mia must be a very good friend!" Cayden said with a grin and wink. "I just need to change and get something we can carry him in. Won't take but a minute. Would you keep an eye on him?"

She came back down in less than five minutes with a box lined with towels. "This should work. Do you mind holding him or should we put him in the back hoping he doesn't jump out?"

With no hesitation, Daniel scooped him up and placed him in the box before settling himself in her car. He gave Cayden directions to the vet office and proceeded to croon to the puppy. "Hey, little buddy, what's your story?"

Cayden started to laugh as she realized both she and Daniel had called the tiny pup by the same name. "It appears our little ward has at least a temporary name – Buddy." And it warmed her heart to think she might have a new furry friend in her new world.

Buddy was diagnosed to be a bit undernourished but otherwise in reasonable health. The vet was happy to send him home with just a few instructions and plans for a return visit on Tuesday. In the meantime, they would canvas the neighborhood to make sure he wasn't someone else's puppy. They made a quick stop at the pet store to pick up needed supplies and toys, of course, before returning to Cayden's apartment.

After seeing to Buddy's needs, Cayden created a leaflet complete with Buddy's photo, which she would distribute in the vicinity of where he had been found after church the next day. It wasn't until this chore was complete and a contented Buddy relaxed in Daniel's lap that she realized she hadn't eaten anything since an early breakfast.

"I'm starved. It's dinnertime and I haven't had lunch. Do you have dinner plans? I could order something or make some omelets. Interested?" she asked as she lifted Buddy into her own lap.

With a sheepish grin, Daniel informed her that he had made a date with Mia for dinner. "It's funny. I stopped by your place on a whim to see if you wanted to grab lunch, which was overridden with taking care of Buddy. Now, because of Buddy, I've reconnected with an old friend and have a dinner date. Wonders never cease! I better get a move on, or I'll be late picking her up." On his way out the door, he offered to help knock on doors passing out leaflets after church, which she gratefully accepted.

After one last pat on Buddy's head, he was gone and somehow the room seemed a little less cozy than it had a few minutes earlier. Cayden brushed the idea aside chalking it up to the fact she needed to eat and settle herself and Buddy in for the night. It had been quite a day and both deserved a good rest.

A sleepy Cayden arrived just in time for Sunday school the next morning. She and Buddy had a bit of a learning curve to living together but she was sure they would work it all out in no time. She just needed to not get too attached just in case he already had a family to love him.

As soon as church services ended, Daniel and Cayden stopped to check on Buddy and enjoy a quick lunch before beginning their task. After knocking on the doors of all houses in the area where Buddy had been found and talking to many of those in the neighborhood, it was obvious that no one knew of a little puppy that had gone on walkabout. Cayden sighed with relief believing that Buddy was safe in his new home.

Life with a puppy took some getting used to with one big adjustment being what could not be left for Buddy to reach and chew on. Anything was fair game for his sharp puppy teeth including rugs, shoes, purses, and furniture legs. Cayden spent most of her time at home loving on him but also a fair amount of time training him. Somehow, the little ball of fur knew to go to the door when he needed to go outside, which was a huge blessing not to have to be constantly cleaning up messes. He quickly learned his name and slowly seemed to realize the meaning of a firm "no."

Any extra effort it took was well worth it because Cayden loved coming home to Buddy's kisses and enjoyed having him to discuss the day's events with as he turned his little head this way and that as if understanding her. Cayden had turned her loneliness over to God and he had brought Buddy into her life. If she had a list of things for which to be thankful, Buddy's name would be at the very top. It surprised her to realize that Daniel's name would not be much further down the list.

# Chapter 16

*J*anuary quickly turned into February and love was in the air. Allie and Rod had been dating since Christmas and they seemed quite smitten with each other. Of course, the romance between Ila and Phillip was deepening and anyone could see they were in love. Phillip's out-of-town speaking engagements limited their time together, but he had assured Ila that he would be home for the young adult sweetheart banquet. While the girls were happy that Phillip was sharing the *Feed My Sheep* ministry with other churches, they hoped his traveling slowed down soon or they would all need to buy new clothes. Ila had been serious about eating ice cream when she was missing him, and she never liked to eat ice cream alone.

Cayden was head of the planning committee for the banquet, which was keeping her busy. That, along with Buddy, didn't leave much time to think about her own state of no romance. But when it did creep into her thoughts, she didn't dwell on the fact there was no one special in her life. Even Marta's recent call announcing she and Wade had finally set a wedding date for August 4 didn't dampen her spirits. She knew that God had kept her from jumping into a relationship with Josh just out of sheer loneliness. She also trusted God to lead her to the man He had for her, if indeed His plan for her life included a husband. For the time being, she was content standing on the sidelines watching her friends enjoy that special time of new love.

The sweetheart banquet was a catered dinner with the youth group acting as wait staff. Decorating the fellowship hall had been fun. She had recruited Beth, Ellen, and Renee to help with the planning and getting everything done. The time spent with her friends was precious to Cayden and their creativity amazed her. By the time they had everything ready, the hall looked like something from a fairy tale. Connor Murphy, a retired Air Force chaplain, would be the guest speaker and Don would be the official master of ceremonies for the evening. He wouldn't let Cayden in on his plans for the evening's program but assured her it would be fun. Her only duty for the evening was to be the official greeter. After that, she was to relax and enjoy the evening.

Greeting everyone turned out to be quite fun. The ladies had enjoyed creating place cards and Cayden gladly directed each person or couple to their table. It was going to be a great evening with good food, fun, and sweet fellowship. Just as that thought flitted through her mind, she looked up to see Daniel and a lovely young woman, who Cayden recognized as Mia from the vet's office, coming through the door. With a quick smile, she welcomed them and indicated their table. She knew Daniel had talked about having a "plus one" for the banquet but it still threw her to see him with someone he had dated in the past and who seemed quite comfortable with him. Not understanding her reaction or why her joy in the evening had dimmed slightly, she determined to reset her mind to the task at hand and have fun. She was just glad the seating arrangements had her at a table across the room from where the couple would be sitting.

As the evening kicked into high gear, Cayden found herself enjoying it immensely. Not knowing the banquet program had been a little scary at first since she was chair of the planning committee; but, in the end, she appreciated Don's insistence to keep her in the dark. It was so much more fun to sit back and let the evening unfold. She even let it roll off her back when she was referred to as "Killer Cayden" during a look back at the past year's class parties. That label might haunt her always!

At the end of the evening, Don asked Phillip to close in prayer. To everyone's surprise, when Phillip accepted the microphone, he took a deep breath and asked Ila to join him on stage. Cayden could tell from the look on Don's face that he knew nothing of what was happening, which made it even more intriguing. As Ila walked up the stage steps, she stopped, placed her hands on her hips and asked in a saucy voice, "Phillip Doucet what are you up to?"

In answer, Phillip waved her toward him and took her hand. "We all have known each other for just a few months; but in those months, you've seen the love Ila and I have for each other grow into something special. So, I thought it only fitting to include you in what is most assuredly the next, and only, step for us." Dropping to one knee, he popped open a ring box and asked her to marry him. For about a millisecond, there was complete stunned silence until Ila screamed her answer "YES!"

What happened next was sort of a blur because first Cayden and Allie rushed forward and then everyone gathered around the couple as Phillip soundly kissed Ila and placed a lovely diamond ring on her left ring finger. There was crying, laughing, hugging, and a lot of "I told you!" amidst the pandemonium. Taking the microphone, Don asked everyone to join hands before he prayed the sweetest prayer for God's blessing on the couple and their life together. Unable to top that, Don grinned and told everyone to have a great rest of their evening.

After things calmed down, Phillip and Ila invited their usual crowd to join them at Olaf's. It was time to celebrate and celebrate they did!

# Chapter 17

*T*he following morning, Cayden thought Ila was going to explode during Jeff's Sunday school lesson. She quickly scribbled a note asking if everything was okay to which Ila replied she needed to have some time with her and Allie. Phillip was leaving after worship service for a Sunday night service in West Virginia and she wanted them to grab lunch and meet at her townhouse. Cayden shared the note with Allie and they both shook their heads in assent. When a huge grin flashed on Ila's face, the other girls let out a deep sigh of relief to know there wasn't anything wrong – Ila just needed to talk with her best friends.

As they suspected, their newly engaged friend was about to pop with pent up joy and so many ideas. Ila and Allie picked up lunch while Cayden dashed home to take care of Buddy. They settled around Ila's dining table and waited for her to begin. Cayden and Allie were surprised when, instead of talking, Ila burst into tears. Not sure which kind of tears were being shed, they continued to wait until Ila took a big gulp of air and smiled the brightest smile imaginable at them.

"There, I didn't realize it but that must have been just what I needed. After I realized what was happening last night, I think my brain and heart went into a sort of dazed shutdown. I'd wanted it and prayed for it but couldn't believe it was really happening. And then all of a sudden, we were swept away with all of you and your loving excitement. Phillip didn't leave here until around two o'clock this morning because we had so much to discuss. This is the first chance I've had to just breathe and let the reality sink in. I'm going to marry Phillip!" she finished with a shout and jumping up grabbed Allie and Cayden in a group hug while they jumped along with her.

Calm was eventually restored, and the conversation began in earnest. She was marrying Phillip and there were a lot of details her best friends needed to know so they could begin helping her get things done.

"You told us not long ago that when Phillip proposed you wouldn't want a long engagement. I'm thinking you guys would have discussed a wedding date. Tell us when it is and we'll make sure everything is just like you want it to be. Are you thinking June? That would give us four months, which isn't much time, but we can do it," Allie said with a grin. Knowing Ila, most of the wedding plans were already firm in her mind and they just needed to get the ball rolling.

"You're right – June isn't much time. So how about March 17?" Ila quickly replied with a grin that also contained a bit of a questioning look because she knew her friends would probably think she was insane.

Cayden didn't bat an eye before replying, "That's a whole year from now. When you said it would be quick, I thought you meant like a month, two months, three months – not a year."

As Ila continued to grin, both Cayden and Allie realized what she was actually saying. Allie was first to find her voice. "You mean this March 17, which is only one month away?!"

"Yep! Hold on before you keel over with shock and let me explain," Ila told them as she pulled out a notebook with lots of scribbled notes and ideas. "Phillip's schedule is jam packed until summer with hardly a weekend at home. When we looked at our calendars last night and began searching for a free weekend, there was only one until mid-July and that one weekend is March 17 and 18."

"Hey, that's also your birthday. That will be a great way to also remember your anniversary. If Phillip forgets one or the other, he'll be in the doghouse for sure!" Cayden commented. "But wait a minute. Didn't you say Phillip's birthday is March 17 too?"

Ila started laughing before shaking her head. "Yep, we share a birthday only eight years apart. How convenient will it be to celebrate our birthdays and anniversary each year with a big party?"

Conversation quickly turned to setting up a timeline of what needed to be done in order to give Ila and Phillip the wedding they wanted. Ila started sharing the plans they had sketched out the night before and one thing was obvious, it might not have all the bells and whistles some brides insisted on, but it would be unique.

"First, Cayden, I need you to check with pastor on the date for both him officiating and use of the church and fellowship hall. We would like a one o'clock reception before the ceremony which will be at three o'clock." Ila was reading through her notes and didn't see the surprised looks passing between her best friends.

"Did you say the reception would be first?" Cayden asked, trying not to sound like the idea was bizarre, which it really seemed to be.

Ila looked up and almost laughed at the looks on their faces. "Yes, and here's why. You know how you're at a wedding and have to wait for photos before the reception can begin?" When the other girls nodded, she continued, "Then, there's the reception and the bride and groom seem to never know when to leave. People need to get home or have plans but try to wait to see the couple off. Having the reception first takes care of all that."

"But what about it's bad luck for the groom to see the bride before the wedding?" Allie asked.

"Well, since we don't believe in that superstition, it doesn't pose a problem," Ila assured her. "Phillip is speaking at a church in Williamsburg that Sunday night. This plan allows for us to arrive in Williamsburg Saturday in time for dinner and a nice evening without a lot of scurrying around. Sunday morning we'll attend church and have the afternoon to relax before he speaks that night. On Monday morning, we fly to Pensacola for a speaking engagement on Tuesday. After that, we'll spend a couple of days in the area before returning home."

Both girls were amazed at Ila's calm. That was a lot of information for them to take in. Cayden wondered aloud, "So, you're quitting your job? You'll be traveling with Phillip?"

Nodding agreement, Ila continued. "I'll give them my two-week notice tomorrow, which will give me time to get my townhouse ready to sell and pack up all my stuff. According to my realtor, it should sell quickly, which brings me to asking a favor. Cayden, if it sells before the wedding, would you mind a houseguest? I can sleep on the couch."

"Of course you can stay with me! I'd be happy to have you. If you need to store anything, I'm sure Don and Beth wouldn't mind you storing it in their garage. I could leave my car out to make the room needed." Cayden was happy to have her friend spend time with her before embarking on this new and exciting chapter of her life.

"That's great and I appreciate it more than you know! Phillip doesn't have a lot of furniture and some of it is rather old. So, we'll see which pieces I have that will go in his apartment. We should be able to fit all of my boxes in Phillip's apartment for the time being and anything else I might store at mom and dad's house, but I'll keep that idea in mind," Ila responded while continuing to peruse her lists. "You'll probably think this is crazy but we're thinking about buying an RV to travel around in and letting Phillip's apartment go. The lease is up in June, which will give us time to consider if that's really what we want to do. One thing we both agree on is that Fredericksburg is our home base with Southside as our home church."

Allie and Cayden were relieved to know that Ila wouldn't just disappear from their lives. While they were thrilled for her, this was going to be hard. The three girls had grown so close and would miss the camaraderie and support they had come to rely on.

As if reading their thoughts, Ila assured them that she would only be a phone call away. She also shared her biggest need and that was to have them back home praying for her as she followed her husband and they shared his ministry together.

Sensing the need to brighten the mood, Ila launched into plans for who would be in the bridal party and what they had decided for the reception. "Of course, since it's St. Patrick's Day, we are going with green and an off-white for the color scheme. I don't want to use green and white because I should be the only one in white," she said cheekily. "Now, for the question I should have started off with – will you both be my maids of honor?" Even taking for granted they would be asked, both girls shrieked a big "Yes!" before Ila continued.

"I'm going to ask Phillip's sister, Penny, to be matron of honor, and he will ask his brother, Paul, to be best man. He's also going to ask Daniel and Luke to be groomsmen. That will take care of the bridal party. Since we're not being traditional, we'll not have a flower girl or ringbearer. But that's not the most unusual thing about this wedding. Instead of a huge outlay of money for flowers, we both decided to take the money we would have spent at the florist and donate it to *Feed My Sheep*. There will be the usual bouquets and boutonnieres but only two arrangements on the platform." She took a break to get everyone hot drinks and to give Cayden and Allie a moment to absorb everything she and Phillip had decided. She counted on them to give their truthful opinions and to chime in if they had helpful ideas.

After delivering hot cocoa, she asked what they thought of her plans thus far and was rewarded with very helpful ideas. They agreed that a small floral budget was a good idea but encouraged her to not skimp on anything to the point that one day she would wish it had been done differently. This was something she had pondered at five o'clock that morning when she woke up and couldn't get back to sleep. She had turned her pondering into prayer asking for peace with everything they were planning to do. Within minutes, she had fallen back into a peaceful sleep. Sharing that information with her friends, seemed to put their minds at ease.

Ila planned to ask Ellen to cater the reception knowing it would be delicious and done right. Ellen's culinary skills and pastries were known far and wide and Ila was going to give her free reign to put her Irish stamp on their reception. She was also going to ask Ellen to determine the type of cake and how to decorate it. The only thing she must have was a trinity knot cake topper.

"Oh, Ellen is going to love that!" Cayden exclaimed. "And it will be spectacular. You've covered most of the basics. What about your dress and the invitations?"

After a brief pause to take a sip of cocoa, Ila filled them in on the dress. "I found a vintage wedding gown a couple of years ago and have it hanging in my closet. I was waiting to get it out until you guys were here with me, even though I was dying to yank the bag out after Phillip left this morning! I'll get it."

Both girls rose as Ila returned with a garment bag over her arm. She had never told them about buying a wedding dress and they were anxious to see what gown could make Ila's face light up in such a way. As she unzipped the bag and the train flowed out, they stepped closer. When they could see the entire dress, they sighed in unison. It was absolutely lovely – not showy or pretentious – just perfection for Ila's tastes. It had long lace sleeves with the same lace covering the bodice. The scooped neckline was feminine and modest and the row of satin buttons on the back added just the right touch of class. A short train fell from the waist in gentle folds that would enhance Ila's natural grace as she walked down the aisle. Oh, their friend had picked the perfect gown and no mistaking it.

Unable to stand the quiet a second longer, Ila blurted, "Well, do you like it?"

Vigorously shaking their heads, they were finally able to speak through the tears. Allie put it into the perfect statement of validation, "This dress may have belonged to someone else in the past, but it was made for you." At that, the three dissolved into tears until Cayden asked if they could see it on Ila, to which she gladly agreed. When she returned to the room in the dress, tears took over again but were soon conquered with shouts of joy. No alterations were needed. It would go to the dry cleaners tomorrow and the dress would be checked off the list.

"Of course, we have to shop for your dresses. I'll ask Penny if she would like to come up next weekend to go shopping with us. Regardless, please keep all day Saturday open for shopping. I need to have something old, something new and something borrowed," she said counting things off on her fingers.

"What about something blue?" Cayden asked.

Tears gathered again in Ila's eyes as she shared the conversation she'd had early that morning with her dad. "I was going over a lot of this with mom on the phone when suddenly she said dad was insisting he needed to talk to me. She handed him the phone and it was quiet until I heard him clear his throat. My dad doesn't cry often. In fact, I've probably only seen him cry three or four times, so that was a big deal. I didn't realize that he has been saving his grandmother's sapphire earrings to give to me for my wedding." Looking around at her friends, she grabbed a tissue box and tossed it their way. "He promises to give them to me the night before the wedding. I was speechless for a couple of reasons. First, he'd kept this a secret and next because he's not overly emotional. Purposely keeping them for when his only daughter marries doesn't seem like his personality, but it obviously is!"

"Okay, we cry 'uncle' – you don't have to keep making us cry!" Allie proclaimed as she grabbed another tissue. "Seriously, Ila, this wedding is going to be absolutely lovely and will be quite unique, just like you and Phillip."

Cayden chimed in, "I agree! Now, let's make lists of what each of us need to get done."

With that, they buckled down to making lists of what must be done and who was assigned each task. By the time for evening service, they were thrilled and just a bit exhausted from joy and tears.

As soon as Cayden arrived back at church that night, she checked Pastor Harwell's schedule for March 16 and 17 and found his day totally free. She penciled in the rehearsal and wedding, mentally checking that off her list. One thing down, a million left to do.

Entering the sanctuary, she found Ila in deep conversation with Ellen and was relieved to see the older woman grinning from ear to ear and jotting down notes. The reception was off to a great start. Looking around, she saw Phillip talking with Daniel and Luke. Both young men were nodding in approval and slapping Phillip on the back.

Cayden tracked down Pastor Harwell and let him know that Ila and Phillip would like to talk with him after service.

"Ah, they must have decided on a date for their wedding. Even if my calendar is booked that day, I'll do my best to make it so that I'm the one to conduct their ceremony. From the look on your face, I'd guess you've already checked my schedule." He winked as he smiled at her. "Watching their courtship has been such joy and a lot of fun. I think Phillip may have his hands full, but Ila is perfect for him and for his ministry. God is so good! Tell them we'll meet in my office as soon as folks clear out." With that, he hurried to join Daniel on the platform as the first song was introduced.

And, just like that, plans were in full swing for a wedding that was only one month away. March 17 would arrive in a blink!

# Chapter 18

Four weeks had never passed as quickly for Cayden. Between dress fittings and bridal showers, the girls were busy helping Ila pack up her townhouse, which lasted only two days on the market before it was under contract. Part of her belongings were moved to Phillip's apartment and things she needed daily were lined up against the living room wall at Cayden's. Stuff she wasn't sure what to do with yet was stored either at her parents' house or in Beth and Don's garage.

The rehearsal dinner was a lively affair held at Olaf's. Since his initial introduction to the restaurant, Phillip had become good friends with Olaf, the owner, who happily closed the main dining room for the evening to host the dinner for "his favorite couple." It wasn't a huge group, but it was a happy group that could certainly eat. Most of them ordered from Olaf's wonderful breakfast menu. Speeches were made and some joyful tears were shed, especially when Ila's dad presented her with his grandmother's earrings. After that, Phillip and Ila thanked everyone and proclaimed it was time to call it a night. They had a wedding to attend tomorrow!

Ellen outdid herself with the reception and the guests weren't shy about telling her so. Cayden heard a lot of comments about how unusual it was to have the reception first and everyone seemed to love the idea. At half-past two, the bridal party excused themselves to freshen up and precisely at three o'clock, the procession began. When the organist played the first chord of the wedding march, Ila's mother stood and was joined by the congregation to watch the lovely bride travel down the aisle on her father's arm to meet her true love at the marriage altar. Tears were flowing down happy faces as Phillip and Ila said their vows, and much laughter erupted as Pastor Harwell had barely finished speaking the words "you may now kiss your bride" when Phillip gathered Ila into his arms for their first kiss as husband and wife.

Just as planned, the couple was on the road to Williamsburg in plenty of time to make their seven o'clock dinner reservations at the Williamsburg Inn. Her parents had surprised them with two nights at the Inn, along with a five-course wedding dinner. Mr. and Mrs. Doucet had officially embarked on the greatest adventure of their lives, and everyone rejoiced with them.

Cayden stuck around to help Ellen and her team of volunteers straighten up and prepare the church for services the following morning. By the time she got home and took care of Buddy's needs, she was ready to put her feet up. Memories of the day floated through her mind as she relaxed with a cup of hot tea, and she pronounced it all so very good.

March had also held a sweet answer to prayers. After faithfully attending morning services for a month and even joining Beth in her Sunday school class a few times, a tearful Paula knocked on Beth's door one Friday night and asked to talk with her. What followed was a sweet time of questions and answers leading to Paula asking Jesus to forgive her of her sins and confessing Him as Lord.

Hearing his wife shouting with tears in her voice brought Don into the room. When he heard the glad news, he quickly called Cayden, who was over in a flash joining in the praise. After a bit, they sat down for coffee while continuing to discuss what had just happened. Before long, Paula jumped up surprising them all.

She blurted out, "I have to tell mom! She needs to know about Jesus too. Can you come home with me and talk with her?"

Don was first to react. "Of course. Let's stop right now and pray she will be in a good frame of mind to talk and that the Holy Spirit will use our words to speak directly to her heart." Beth reached for Paula's hand and a circle of believers was quickly formed as they all prayed that Mrs. Virginia would understand and accept Jesus into her heart.

They decided that only Don and Beth would go home with Paula and share the Gospel with Paula's mom. Cayden promised to send those on the church prayer chain a text asking them to pray also. By the time, Don, Beth and Paula sat down to talk with Mrs. Virginia, over 100 Christians were praying on her behalf, asking that she be in a good state of mind and that she would accept the gift of salvation.

Cayden had gone home awaiting news when there was a knock on her door. Thinking it might be Beth, she quickly opened the door and was surprised to find Daniel standing there with a pizza box in his hands.

"Hey, hope you don't mind but I didn't want to wait at the house to get news of Mrs. Virginia. Anything yet?" he asked as she let him in the door. "I was shouting and praising all the way here that Paula accepted Christ. You must be over the moon!"

Glad to have someone to continue rejoicing with, Cayden chose not to dissect Daniel appearing on her doorstep and just enjoy his company. "We all are. I can't wait to talk with Paula, but we have eternity for that. So, Mr. Garrett, tell me – is that really pizza in that box because I am starved. I was about to run out and grab something for supper when Don called, and I rushed next door."

They were just finishing pizza and a quickly prepared tossed salad when Ellen arrived. She, too, couldn't stand to wait on news and had thrown together a goody tray before heading to Cayden's to wait. When Allie and Rod dropped by for news, they decided it was time to move next door. When Don and Beth returned home, they were happily surprised to find a party happening in their family room.

Don quickly told them what they'd been praying to hear. "Mrs. Virginia's mind was clear as a bell when we arrived. Paula was so excited she hugged her mom and started sharing her good news. At first, Mrs. Virginia looked shocked and then a huge smile crossed her face." Don stopped to take a sip of tea and Beth picked up the story.

"Paula didn't know that her mom was raised in a Christian home but that Paula's father demanded she not share her faith with their children. So, when Paula told her mother how she had accepted Jesus as her Savior, Mrs. Virginia not only understood but was thrilled. She grabbed Paula in a bear hug and wept tears of joy. As we talked, Don asked leading questions that made us both confident she knows the Lord too." Beth was overtaken with tears of happiness at the goodness of God and His never-ending love.

Realizing Don and Beth hadn't eaten, Cayden ordered lots of pizza because she was sure this party was going to go on for a while. She and Allie made more tea, grabbed paper products and rejoined the group. There was nothing better than praising the Father – especially when they were thanking Him for saving their friend.

# Chapter 19

The month of March had come in like a lamb and, true to the adage, it went out like a lion. Temperatures steadily fell overnight on the last Friday of the month and Cayden awoke Saturday morning to three inches of snow and gusting winds. Happy to relax in her cozy apartment, she set out the ingredients to make her grandmother's recipe for chicken and rice soup. A cold, dreary day called for something hot, nourishing, and comforting, which always made her think of this recipe.

She had just changed into jeans and a sweatshirt when Buddy started whining at the door. This was quickly followed with Don's signature knock, which changed Buddy's whines to yips of excitement. Cayden invited Don in and offered him a cup of coffee, but he indicated the need to get a move on in order to open the shop on time.

"Sorry to bother you, Cayden, but I wanted you to know the steps are all clear and that I've put down rock salt to melt any ice. It's supposed to start warming up before lunchtime and most of this should be gone by tomorrow evening, but still be careful on the steps and the sidewalks – there may be some slick spots." Don stopped to take a breath and to scratch Buddy behind the ears before continuing. "I wonder if you might check on Beth later this morning. She's not feeling the best today."

Cayden picked up on the worry in his voice and asked if he thought it could be the flu so many at church were down with. "If you think she would be up to eating soup, I'll take some over for lunch and visit for a while if she's up to it."

"That would be just what this doctor ordered – soup and a visit with you. If you knock on the door and she's slow to answer, use your key and go on in. Knowing you'll be checking on her will ease my mind. I should be home by four o'clock. Thanks, Cayden." And with that he was out the door.

Replaying what had just occurred, Cayden realized Don hadn't answered if Beth was sick or what the problem was. Glancing at the clock, she realized she had better get busy making the soup so that it would be ready by lunchtime. As she worked, she found her mind wandering back over what Don had or hadn't said and more than once she asked the Father to comfort and heal her friend.

After packing soup, crackers, and chocolate chip cookies in her thermal backpack, Cayden dressed warmly for the short trip next door. Even though temperatures were a little warmer, it was still bitter out there. Buddy ran around her to let her know he would like to go also. She debated and finally decided Beth might enjoy a visit from both of them. She and Don babysat Buddy and sometimes even came over to get him while she was at work so he could spend time with them. Beth called him her "best bud." So, maybe, her best bud would be a good dose of medicine for whatever ailed her.

Cayden put the backpack on her back and scooped Buddy up under her arm. Heeding Don's warning, she was careful going down the steps and avoided slick spots on the way next door. She rang the bell and even knocked with no reply. Using her key, she opened the door and called out but still nothing. She put Buddy down and followed his excited yips to the downstairs family room. When she entered the room, she found Beth sitting in a chair with her head in her hands weeping. Buddy was sitting at her feet.

Not knowing what else to do, Cayden knelt in front of Beth and quietly asked if she was all right. "Beth, what can I do to help? Are you feeling ill?"

It was a couple of minutes before Beth's weeping lessened and she was able to talk. Lifting her head, she gave Cayden a half-smile and squeezed her hand before speaking. "Don asked you to check on me, didn't he? He wanted to stay home to be with me, but I needed time alone."

Realizing her visit might be an intrusion, Cayden told her about her conversation with Don and indicated she'd brought lunch over. She took both of Beth's hands and asked if she could pray with her before she went back home so that Beth could have the time she needed.

"Oh, no, dear girl, don't leave. God knew I needed you and my best bud and here you are." Trying to stop the stream of tears, Beth gave an unsteady smile. "To put your mind at ease, I'm not ill just sad."

Cayden got up and retrieved a chair to sit beside her friend. "If you would like to talk, I'm glad to be here for you and listen. If instead you just need me to sit here quietly with you, I can do that too."

Taking a shuddering breath, Beth nodded and again bowed her head. "You know Don and I have no children. What you probably don't know is that we did have a baby girl, Annie, and today would have been her twenty-fifth birthday." Even though tears continued to flow, Beth's face lit up with just the mention of her baby. "The doctors thought we would never conceive so you can imagine our surprise when a pregnancy test came up positive. I still refused to believe it until I'd gone to my doctor, and she confirmed I was indeed three months pregnant. Don took such tender care of me, and we did everything the doctors told us to make sure our baby would be healthy."

Beth got up and looked out the window at the snow and gray clouds. "The weather was exactly the opposite of today. It was sunny and the temperature was in the sixties. It was a Wednesday and Don had taken off to go to a doctor appointment with me. I was eight months along and things seemed fine." Sniffling and folding her arms over her chest, she continued. "The doctor wasn't happy with the baby's heartbeat and sent me directly to the hospital. As we walked into the emergency room, my water broke. I'm a little blurry about what happened next. Contractions began strong and hard, one after the other. There was no time for them to give me anything or to try and slow the process down. Annie was born thirty minutes after my arrival at the hospital."

It seemed to Cayden that Beth was no longer telling her story but reliving it. She looked up and for the first time seemed to actually see Cayden. While tears were still falling, a sweet smile lifted the corners of her mouth and her eyes lit up as she continued. "They told us we had a little girl, and little she was weighing in at exactly five pounds. She gave the sweetest little cry before they whisked her across the room to an incubator and to check her over. In the meantime, my doctor was working on me to stop the bleeding. Poor Don – he was torn between going over to see what was happening with our daughter and staying with me. He may have had the hardest job that day, trying to figure out what to do when there was really nothing anyone could do."

Beth sat on the loveseat near the fireplace and Cayden joined her putting her arm around her shoulders. As Beth laid her head on Cayden's shoulder, she continued her story. "I was rushed to surgery where the only way to save me was to perform a hysterectomy. When I woke up, Don and our pastor were with me, and I knew there must be problems with our baby. They explained that her little heart wasn't completely formed and there was nothing the doctors could do for her. Cayden, I had never felt God's presence with me more than at that moment in time. Don says I was regal as a queen when I struggled to sit up and demanded in a kind voice that they bring my baby to me." Beth stopped again and smiled. "Don left the room and within minutes I was holding my child. She was beautiful and so perfect with her tiny fingers and toes and crop of golden hair. As I took her little hand, she curled her fingers around my index finger and opened her eyes looking straight into mine. That was the most precious moment of my life as I looked deep into my baby's eyes and caught a glimpse of heaven. Don or I held her for the next hour before she closed her beautiful eyes and joined Jesus."

Cayden was openly weeping while also praising the Lord for letting her friend have this precious memory of her sweet girl. "And you named her Annie? Had you already picked her name?"

Beth sighed, "She was always Annie, named after my grandmother. I often think of Grandma holding my little Annie and maybe telling her something about me. Some people have asked if the pain was too much to bear and I have to say that at times it almost swallowed me up. But, when I remember my hour with Annie and God, I know I wouldn't trade it for anything. He allowed me to be mother to the sweetest baby girl ever, who could not want that?"

A knock on the door brought both women out of their world where Annie was so present with them, and Cayden rose to see who it was. She returned downstairs with Ellen, who had also brought over lunch and who knew her friend would need her on this day. She went to Beth, and they shared a hug and some tears before Ellen announced in a firm voice that it was time to eat. This brought a real smile to Beth's face, as she nodded agreement.

Beth went upstairs to freshen up as the others put out a hearty, cold-weather day lunch of soup, chicken salad sandwiches, and several dessert offerings. As they worked, Ellen quietly explained that she always tried to spend some time with Beth on Annie's birthday. She and her late husband had been friends with Don and Beth when Annie was born and had done what they could to help them through the hard times.

Just as Beth was entering the breakfast nook, she heard Ellen tell Cayden how thankful she was to have her in their lives. "I second that emotion," she said with a bit of her old self shining through. "You have been such a blessing to us Cayden. I wrote your mom a note just last week thanking her for sharing you with us. When God led you to Don's garage that day, I know you think it was for you – and it was – but it was for us too." With that, she hugged Cayden, sat down, and said, "What's to eat? I'm starved!"

# Chapter 20

Southside Baptist had launched its *Feed My Sheep* ministry in January. Connor Murphy had volunteered to oversee the ministry. As a retired Air Force chaplain, he was the perfect candidate. His love for the Lord and his people skills fitted him for the task of managing a large group of volunteers to most effectively run the program and work with those they ministered to. Over thirty volunteers had attended a training session Phillip conducted in late December and they were ready to get things going.

The decision was to start off with just one Saturday each month for the first five or six months to get a feel for how the program was received and to know how much food and supplies would be needed. Cayden had volunteered and Connor quickly adopted her as his administrative right-hand. In addition to helping on Saturdays, she was also active in the behind-the-scenes activities preparing for serving those who responded to their invitation for a hot meal and Bible lesson in the church gymnasium.

Ellen coordinated volunteers and schedules for providing meals. Renee and her husband, Richard, worked with some of the local charities to accumulate a stockpile of clothes. Volunteers cleaned, mended, and tagged the clothes with sizes to share them at the end of each service. Amy Hawkins, who had previous experience in a similar program at her home church in Richmond, was happy to take over the responsibility of accumulating soaps, shampoos, socks, combs, etc. to make up essentials kits to be shared.

Connor had recruited Allie to lead the Welcome Team, which she was perfect for with her sunny disposition and sweet heart. Luke and others were on this team, and they met at least once each week to pray and ask God for guidance not just for their team but for all those involved. They prayed especially for those they were ministering to as they were fed a healthy, tasty meal and heard a message straight from God's Word explaining how they could know Jesus as their Savior.

Amy's husband, Landon, led the team of van drivers who would be at certain locations as advertised to transport people to and from the church. Daniel had volunteered for this team, along with four other men in the church. Phillip had spent extra time with this team to offer tips on what to expect and how to handle tricky situations.

Connor met weekly with team leaders and all volunteers to encourage them and to make sure all needs were being met. He took care of advertising, including newspaper ads, leaflets, and radio ads. It was a lot to keep track of and Cayden did what she could to lessen his load. She kept spreadsheets on all team activities and schedules of who was doing what on each Saturday. She worked with Austin, one of the deacons at Southside and a member of Gideons International, to procure Bibles to be included in gift bags for those attending for the first time. She also recorded attendance along with whatever personal information people were willing to share.

Pastor Harwell led a team of speakers consisting of himself, Connor, Austin, and Daniel. They rotated so that there would be different speakers, including Phillip when he was in town. He appointed Micah Sparrow to lead a team of soul winners to share the message of salvation with anyone who came forward during the invitation. Micah's love for the Lord and for seeing others accept Christ was evident to anyone who talked with him for any length of time.

As Phillip had described, some came out of curiosity, some for free food, and others just to have something to do. But none left without hearing the message of salvation. God promised His Word would not return until Him void and the following weeks proved that true. No one answered altar call the first Saturday; but in February, seven people accepted Christ. *Feed My Sheep* at Southside was in full swing, and everyone involved received blessing after blessing for their hard work and dedicated prayers.

Cayden came home most days mentally tired but happy. It was hard to believe that back in July she was worried about being lonely and not having a purpose. She had taken her mom's wise advice and look where she was now. She had made so many new friends both at church and in the neighborhood and she was excited to be part of several ministries. Of course, there was

Buddy, who filled up the room and her heart with his sweet disposition. With him around, she would never be lonely. She couldn't help but rejoice. Life was more than good – it was grand!

# Chapter 21

Warmer temperatures and bright sunshine ushered in the month of May. People were moving outdoors, working in their yards, taking walks, or just sitting on their porches soaking up the sun. Cayden was happy that Allie liked to join her for Saturday morning bike trips and she was teaching Allie tennis. Since basketball was Allie's favorite sport, she thought it only fair that they occasionally spent time shooting baskets at the local YMCA.

Rod had accepted a job as a ski instructor at a ski lodge in Colorado since the Virginia ski season was over. Although he and Allie spoke often, Allie had to admit she didn't care for a long-distance relationship. This, combined with the possibility he might relocate out west, didn't bode well for the couple. Over milkshakes one Sunday night, she told Cayden they had decided to just be friends.

"Hey, who can't use more friends, right?" she joked, with only a touch of sadness in her eyes. "I really don't see how Marta stands being thousands of miles away from Wade. A long-distance relationship isn't something I think my heart can handle. And I'm not like Ila, who knew she wanted to marry and even had the kind of man she preferred down pat. I'm not unhappy being single, but I must admit flirting with the idea of love was fun while it lasted. I mean the special attention, the butterflies when he walked in a room or I saw his name on my phone, and the flowers were great; but in the end, we weren't on the same page with where we wanted our lives to go. I'm a homebody with simple tastes and a desire to not stray too far from my family. Rod's a free spirit, ready to jump on a plane at a moment's notice to do something exciting and fun. One thing though that we had in common was our love for the Lord and that was special. I'll miss my friend but I'm happy with my life and I'll be even happier in a month when school is out!" she ended with a grin.

"So, do you have any big plans for the summer? I haven't taken hardly any time off since I started work at the church. It would be fun to do something together – go somewhere fun – do something new. What do you think?" Cayden asked as her excitement for the prospect began to grow. "I can't afford anything too extravagant but a trip somewhere neither of us has visited before would be cool."

Catching the excitement, Allie added, "Let's rent a convertible, pick a major highway and just start driving. Or is that just too spontaneous and wild?"

"Depends. Would you want to go south, north or west because we can't really go any further east." Cayden chuckled as she finished her shake. "I like the idea of west and I would love renting a convertible. I've only been as far west as Ohio."

Allie gave it a thought and Cayden could see the wheels of her mind turning as a grin crossed her face. "We both got excited when the Jacobs family came back from Ark Encounter in Kentucky so enthusiastic about their trip. We could visit that and the Creation Museum. What could be next?"

Cayden was busily pulling up a map of the United States on her phone. "Well, after watching Downton Abbey, I've been wanting to tour the Biltmore Estate in Asheville. It would be great if we could work that into our itinerary. Oh, and I don't think Dollywood is all that far from Asheville. That's somewhere our family talked about going but never got around to visiting and I think the whole area around the park has developed into a true vacation spot with tons of things to do in Pigeon Forge and Gatlinburg. Would that interest you at all?"

"I'm loving it! School will be out June 1 and I'll be free to leave any time after that. How about we leave on Saturday, June 9, and plan to be gone the entire next week? Would that work with your schedule?" As Allie spoke her voice began to rise in excitement. "Other than 4-H trips and some family vacations, I haven't been many places. Please say you can do it!"

Looking up from her phone, Cayden agreed, "I just checked my calendar, and that week is perfect. I hope you don't mind but there is one thing I prefer. The planner part of me really would like to at least have a loose itinerary so that we know we have tickets and hotel rooms booked. The idea of driving through areas where we can't find a decent hotel is not appealing and I think our parents wouldn't care for that either. Would that be okay?"

Allie started to laugh before she quickly agreed. "After all, sometimes the planning of a trip can be as fun as the actual vacation. We can both start exploring the best routes and what interesting sights we can see. Want to meet up tomorrow after work and get started? The sooner the reservations are made, the sooner we can pack bags knowing where we're going. This is going to be a blast!"

Pastor Harwell had been happy to approve Cayden's request for the week off and Beth and Don were happy to have Buddy stay with them while she would be away. Also, Don insisted he use his garage connections to get them a dependable, yet sharp, convertible for their road trip. All that was left was to make their plans and enjoy a much earned, much anticipated vacation.

They met at Cayden's apartment two days later and shared what they had already learned before searching the internet for ideas. An itinerary and route were agreed upon with sights to see along the way noted. Since the end of the school year was going to be quite hectic, Allie was happy when Cayden volunteered to make hotel reservations and check on ticket prices. By the time they were ready to call it a night, their plans were pretty much firmly in place and they were over the moon excited.

For Cayden, the trip was significant for a couple of reasons. She would have just completed a year out of school, a year living on her own in Fredericksburg, and a year in her job at Southside. A road trip of sorts had been the catalyst for some of those things and now she would celebrate all those milestones with a road trip with her best friend. What could be better?

A few days later, Marta called with another big announcement. Wade had accepted a job as Chief Electrical Engineer for the City of Joslin, Delaware, with a nice pay raise, and they had decided she could go ahead and put in her notice at work. It would help being at home as she made final wedding preparations, and it would give her some time to wind down before the big day. She would be back in Winchester before Memorial Day.

Both girls were excited knowing they would soon once again be only about two hours apart. When Cayden asked about her job, Marta explained, "At first, I felt terrible to have only been in the job for five months before leaving but there's a local pastor's wife who has been volunteering and hoping the work would eventually turn into a full-time position. So, they have offered the job to her, and she'll be shadowing me until I leave."

In unison, the girls repeated their favorite phrase, "God is good all the time and all the time God is Good!"

Marta filled Cayden in on anything new pertaining to the wedding. In response to Cayden asking how Wade was handling all the wedding "stuff," Marta laughed before explaining his plans to help a college roommate move to Pensacola during the second week in June. "He thinks he's fooling me when he acts pitiful about driving a rental truck from Lynchburg to Florida and back. But I know it looks better to him than sticking around home for endless discussions he'd rather not be a part of."

A light bulb went off in Cayden's head, prompting her to ask, "When did you say he's going to be out of town?"

"I think they'll leave sometime on June 8 and be gone for several days. He's taking the following week off since he has plenty of vacation built up. I told him to enjoy the road trip with Jake – one last all boys' vacation."

Cayden was getting excited about her new idea but wanted to talk to Allie before mentioning it to Marta. "Hey, can I call you back in the morning? Buddy needs to go out." And with that the conversation ended so that Cayden could call Allie as she took Buddy out for the last time that night.

With a definite green light from Allie, Cayden called Marta on her morning break to pose a question. "Would you like to join Allie and me on a road trip? It's the same timeframe Wade will be out of town, which is amazing if you ask me, or one might even call it *providential*."

After filling Marta in on all their plans and reassuring her that Allie was happy to have her join them, Cayden expected time would be needed to check with Wade and make sure things would run smoothly without her. But, instead, she heard a loud "Whoop!" followed by a "Thank you, Jesus!" from Marta. "I truly believe some time to unwind with you girls is an answer to prayers. The last six months have been filled with moving to Texas, learning a new job, finding a church, all while planning our wedding. I was hoping to find something that would give me even a small break – maybe a day at a spa but this is perfect. Count me in! I can't wait to spend time with you and to get to know Allie."

And, just like that, Cayden remembered thinking earlier "what could be better?" She now knew the answer – a road trip with not one but two sweet friends.

115

# Chapter 22

*D*aniel came into the office the following week with a spring in his step. Cayden noticed it and wondered if it had anything to do with Mia. They had been a pretty regular item since rekindling their relationship. The thought bothered her even though she really didn't get why. Mia was pleasant and she certainly had been kind to her and Buddy. They seemed well suited but she didn't want Daniel to jump too quickly into something more serious. That was it – she was just concerned for Daniel's welfare. Clearing her throat she asked, "What's gotten into you today? You've been humming and almost grinning since you arrived. Spill the beans, buster!"

Grinning at her, he shared some big news. "Well, if you must know, I've been asked to preach at a church in Aylett this coming Sunday morning and evening."

"Oh, that's cool, but hardly big news. You preach at other churches from time to time and don't get quite as excited about it as this. What's different?" she asked as she continued going over Sunday's bulletin.

"Their pastor is retiring, and they are looking for a new pastor. The head deacon called to say I'm one of the candidates they're interested in to possibly fill the vacancy. He asked me to pray about it and let him know if it was something I would be interested in. So, I've prayed and feel it's definitely what God would have me do. It may not turn out to be anything more than a chance to share the Gospel, but it could open the door for a full-time pastor position." He seemed to be working to contain his enthusiasm as he spoke. "This is the first time for me to be invited as a candidate for pastor of a church and I'm about to pop. Add to that the fact Aylett is less than an hour from my family, friends, and my home and it's an awesome opportunity. In talking with the deacon, I found out the church is small but has seen recent growth and he expects that trend to continue."

Happy for Daniel, Cayden smiled and congratulated him. "I'm proud of you and I'll be praying God's will in this big opportunity. They would be quite blessed to have you as their pastor." As she finished speaking, she realized it would mean he would no longer work or worship at Southside and the thought made her a bit sad. It surprised her to think that she would really miss him. Pushing sadness away, she returned to work as Daniel went down the hallway whistling.

The next Saturday morning, Cayden decided to do a good spring cleaning in her apartment. Of course, it wouldn't take very long since it wasn't very big. But it still necessitated moving things around, and having Buddy underfoot wouldn't be smart. So, she took him down to the garage where Don was working on his car and put him in the fenced area Don had set up for him a few weeks earlier. That way, he would enjoy Don's company and get some fresh air while she worked. It was a win-win situation for all of them.

A couple of hours later, Don came up to say he and Beth were going to run some errands and reminded her Buddy was in his play area. He had closed the bay doors, but the side door was open to let a breeze come through. Realizing it was about time he would be needing to go outside, she hurried to finish her chores.

Happy to have her apartment cleaned from top to bottom, she changed so that she and Buddy could take a walk before coming back for lunch. She grabbed his leash and hummed to herself as she went down the steps and into the garage. Knowing he would have heard her, she thought he must have fallen asleep because otherwise he would have been barking a welcome greeting. But when she looked at his play area, it was empty. Thinking he had to be somewhere in the garage, she searched and called his name only to realize he was nowhere to be found. The last time she put him in the play area, he had tried to climb out but it was too tall. Maybe his little puppy legs had grown enough and he had been tenacious enough to climb to freedom. But where was he?

Panic was building as Cayden ran out calling his name and listening for him but there was nothing. She checked all around Beth and Don's house and property and no Buddy. Thinking it might be best to drive around the neighborhood, she ran upstairs to get her purse and keys, all the while trying to figure out the best plan. Buddy hadn't been off leash outside and wouldn't know how to behave. She had to think quickly of what to do. She tried Beth and Don's phones but got no answer. Before she gave it another thought, she was dialing Daniel, who picked up on first ring.

Without even saying hello, she filled him in on what had happened and asked if he could help look for Buddy. "I hate to mess up any plans you have and will understand if you say no but I couldn't think of who else to call."

Hearing tears and fear in her voice, he quickly assured her he was on his way. "I'm only about five minutes away. Why don't you walk over to Paula's, and I'll meet you there? Don't panic. We'll find him." And with that, he hung up.

Cayden took off toward Paula's farm, calling and whistling for Buddy. By the time she reached Paula's house, she was in tears and could hardly speak to explain what was going on when Paula answered the door. She immediately came out and joined Cayden in searching. Paula headed to the barn and Cayden went toward the horse paddock. They had just met back up on the front porch when Daniel arrived. Cayden ran to the Jeep and jumped in as she thanked Paula for her help.

"I don't know what to do next," she cried. "He's not used to being loose and he wouldn't know to stay out of the road. Where can we check next?"

Gently taking her hands, Daniel bowed his head and prayed for guidance and for Buddy's safety. He then formulated a plan where he would drive slowly, and she would look and call for Buddy. The first place they would go would be back to the area where Buddy had found Cayden. Perhaps his doggie senses would have remembered the area. It was as good a place to start as anywhere else. They called and whistled but to no avail – there was no sign of him. Several of the neighbors heard them calling out and joined in the search. Cayden quickly jotted down her cell phone number and gave it to a woman who seemed to take charge and promised to call if they saw Buddy.

Leaving that area meant getting out on roads that were busier than inside a neighborhood, which meant driving slowly wasn't a real option. Cayden scanned as quickly as possible the roadways and yards continually yelling his name. At an intersection about a mile from her apartment, she was scanning the yards to the right when Daniel suddenly stopped, threw the Jeep into park and bolted out the door. Looking his way, she spotted something small by the stop sign and jumped out to join Daniel. By the time she reached him, Daniel was taking off his sweatshirt, gently laying Buddy on.

"He's hurt but he's alive. We need to get him to the vet. You drive. I'll hold him." Daniel was quickly calling out instructions and Cayden was just as quickly following them. They made it to the emergency vet's office in record time and were ushered to an exam room where the situation had quickly been assessed. Laying Buddy gently on an exam table, Daniel stepped aside to provide room for the vet team to work. That was when Cayden saw the blood on his t-shirt and her fears kicked into high gear. She hadn't had time to really process what had happened to Buddy or how badly he was hurt as she drove to the vet's office. When she looked up, she saw Daniel watching her to make sure she was okay. He had known all along how badly Buddy was injured but shielded her from it by holding him instead of giving him to her. There were tears in his eyes as he opened his arms and held her while she sobbed.

The vet was kind but succinct when he ordered them out of the room. "I believe he's been hit by a car and has sustained internal injuries, but I need to take x-rays before we'll know the extent of damage. Right now, I need you to wait in the reception area and let me work."

Knowing he was right and not wanting to impede progress, they left the room and stood just outside in the hallway. She had calmed down and was no longer sobbing but was still weeping. "How careless of me to not have brought him back upstairs when Don left. I should have known he would keep trying to climb over the fence. It's all my fault." She slid down the wall and sat with her head in her hands while hot tears dripped onto her knees. He sat down beside her and placed his hand on her head before again praying for Buddy. After a few minutes, he helped her up and they walked to the waiting room. Daniel excused himself and went to his Jeep to find a clean shirt and two bottles of water. Returning, he saw that Cayden was calmer and just looked dazed. He handed her a bottle of water and they settled in to wait.

While outside, he had texted Don and Beth, who had responded they were on their way to join them. When they came through the door, Cayden began weeping again and Beth took her outside while Don joined Daniel. Don was kicking himself for leaving Buddy alone and Daniel pointed out there was no reason not to as they had done it before with no problem. Now, they knew he was a little escape artist, and a sturdier, taller play area would have to be built. Making plans to build something helped both men divert their worries to something positive they could do.

They had been waiting about thirty minutes when the vet came out and updated them on Buddy's injuries. He had a bad gash on his head and some internal bruising but nothing life threatening. He was concussed and they were waiting for him to rouse, which hopefully would be soon. "It could have been a lot worse – he's one lucky little guy. I think we'll keep him with us until Monday morning to see how he does. For now, it might help to have someone he loves talking to him as he wakes up." With that, he stood and looked at Cayden. "Come on, mama, it will help your boy to hear your voice and I believe it'll help you too."

Not needing to be told twice, Cayden hurried alongside the vet. When she saw her precious little pup lying so still and with bandages on his head, the tears threatened to choke her. The assistant was quick to pull up a chair for her right beside the bed and to hand her a box of tissues before quietly telling her she could gently pet Buddy's side. She sat talking to him, calling him sweet names, and telling him how sorry she was he had been hurt. In about ten minutes, his little eyes opened and stared into hers. A slight moaning sound came from deep in his throat when he tried to move, and the assistant quickly summoned the vet.

"I knew his mama's voice would make all the difference," he pronounced as he administered a shot. "Now that he's awake, we can give him something for the pain. It won't knock him out, but it will help make him comfortable. You can stay another few minutes but then we need him to rest. I know it's not easy but that's what is best for him. We will monitor him through the night and tomorrow to make sure he's doing well. My assistant will call you in the morning to let you know how he's doing." As he was leaving the room, he gave Cayden's shoulder a squeeze. "Hang in there. You've got a lot of years with this tough little guy, and it'll be sprinkled with trying times, but I promise those will not outweigh the good times you have together."

Leaving Buddy was one of the hardest things she had ever done. But her tears had stopped, and her eyes were clear as she joined the others in the waiting room. She updated them on Buddy's condition and the doctor's instructions as they walked to the parking lot. Don was going to suggest Cayden ride home with them; but before he could speak, Daniel had opened the Jeep door for her to join him and she climbed in. Daniel needed to know Cayden was okay and Cayden needed Daniel's strength for a few more minutes, but neither of them realized what that might mean.

# Chapter 23

When Daniel got back home, it seemed like he'd been gone forever but it was only four o'clock. After a hot shower and a cold glass of tea, he settled in to go over his outline for the sermons he would preach at Aylett Baptist the next day. He spent much time in prayer until he heard his stomach growling and realized it was indeed time for dinner.

As he warmed up leftovers from the night before and sat down to eat, his mind flew back over what all had happened. His original intent for the day was to play softball with the church team, do some grocery shopping, study, and maybe call Mia to see if she wanted to have dinner with him. Then, Cayden called and everything else was forgotten. While it was easy for him to rationalize that he had dropped everything because Buddy was involved, he knew that wasn't true. What was true came as a shock. When he heard her voice and knew she needed help, he would have moved heaven and earth to get to her. In fact, he sort of did just that because he drove faster than was advisable and was very glad no police cruisers were around. What should have been at least a ten-minute trip took only five. All he knew was Cayden needed him.

He remembered this same feeling after they had spent the day baking cheesecakes for the ladies' Christmas dinner. His thoughts had led to the decision he needed to talk to God and then to his oldest sister, Julie. "Well," he thought, "no time like the present." On his knees he prayed for wisdom to understand his feelings and to know how to proceed always in God's will.

Julie lived in Hampton with her husband, James, and their two children – Caleb, an active eight-year-old with red hair like his mother, and Marnie, a precocious kindergartner who loves her Uncle Daniel more than anyone. Being ten years older than Daniel, Julie often found herself mothering her only brother from the day he was born and planned to continue as long as he allowed it. So, when he called, she always found time to listen carefully to what he had to say as well as to determine just exactly what he was leaving out. This was why Daniel needed her wise counsel where Cayden was concerned.

She had just gotten Marnie out of the bath and was towel drying her hair when the phone rang. Seeing Daniel's number on the screen, she passed the job over to James and found a comfortable seat in their study. It was quite often the only place where quiet could be found in their house. Happy to talk with "the baby" as she still thought of him, she answered with a cheery, "Hello, brother mine! How are you?"

"Quite well, thanks, and you? I imagine you're getting everyone sorted out with baths and setting out clothes for church tomorrow. Hope you aren't too busy to talk for a few minutes." Daniel knew this was just a polite formality because she would never put him off if she could possibly help it.

Proving him right, she assured him, "There's no one I'd rather talk to right now than you. Mom told me about your opportunity to preach at a church tomorrow with the possibility of maybe being called as pastor. James and I are praying for you and for clear direction. I may be biased, but I know they couldn't get a better man in their pulpit. But, somehow, I don't think that's why you've called." Even though he couldn't see her, he could hear a smile in her voice, which warmed his heart and put him at ease to speak honestly with her.

After he shared what was on his mind and asked his questions, she had only given one piece of advice and that was to listen to his heart and take what it's saying to the Lord. When he asked her to describe what falling in love felt like, she laughed or really it was more of a giggle.

"Ah, for me, it was the sweetest feeling like you might have when falling into the softest pile of feathers while at the same time feeling like you're about to parachute from a plane and you have to decide whether or not to jump. The sweet feeling was easy and such bliss but the jumping out of a plane feeling was a bit terrifying even though it was something I wanted to do more than anything because I knew that once I jumped there was no turning back.

During that time between the faint niggling of love and the bold realization of it, James was on my mind more and more and I found myself eager to be around him and to talk to him. Of course, every person is different, and every relationship is unique but you're a smart boy. You'll know. After all, you were smart enough to call your big sister," she ended with a chuckle and a deep sigh. "You do have one caveat that I didn't have when considering a mate. As a preacher and hopefully one day a pastor, your choice of a wife must meet standards to match your calling. The great thing about God, though, is that if you're following His will, He will never lead you to love someone unsuited to being a preacher's wife."

After a short silence, she asked, "So, tell me, little brother, if this is just a curious question or is there someone in particular you're thinking about? Mom told me you and Mia have been dating again. Is it getting serious?"

"I'm enjoying getting reacquainted with Mia but we're just friends and I think we both know it. There might be someone. I just need to know if what I've only now started to see happening is love. One thing I can say without hesitation is she would be a wonderful preacher's wife. She loves the Lord, is dedicated to His service, has a heart for seeing others come to know Him, and is a precious person." He ended the description of Cayden with a sweet tone that made Julie sit up and take notice.

"Daniel, why don't we stop and pray right now? Because, brother, I think from just listening to you describe her, you're a goner." Julie didn't wait for a reply but immediately prayed for God to lead Daniel in his choice of a wife and that God would also be working in the young lady's heart if it be His will they marry. She ended the prayer and quietly reminded him how much he was loved before saying, "And I'm not going to ask who she is but next time you better be ready to fill me in on all the details!"

When Daniel said good night and disconnected the call, he felt more at ease. From what Julie had said, he might well be in that "faint niggling of love" stage. Even though how he reacted to Cayden today seemed to be heading to the "bold realization" Julie had described. The best part was knowing his Heavenly Father was working all these things for his good and he could trust in that.

He was up earlier than usual Sunday morning preparing himself for the Lord's Day and preaching His Word. His sermons were ready, and he had just sat down to eat breakfast when the phone rang. After all the talk of love last night, his heart seemed to skip a beat when he saw it was Cayden calling.

Surprised but happy, he answered, "Good morning! What's got you up so early this morning? Buddy, okay?"

"Sorry, I didn't mean to scare you. I'm waiting on a call from the vet's assistant and promise to text you as soon as I know what's happening. I just wanted to tell you I've been praying for you and will continue to pray as you go through services today. You'll do just fine, and God will use your words to speak to hearts," she assured him.

"Thanks for praying. I'm ready with what He's laid on my heart to share with the good people of Aylett Baptist. Thought I'd leave plenty early just in case traffic backs up and to give myself time to relax before meeting with the deacons. Were you able to get any sleep last night? I know how much you're worried about Buddy, and I've continued praying for both of you. Like the doctor said, Buddy will be just fine," he said with conviction in his voice.

When she spoke this time, her voice was a bit lighter than before. "You were my lifesaver yesterday and my anchor all at the same time. Not sure how that can be since one lifts you up and the other holds you down but that's how I think of your kindness to Buddy and me. It was only after I'd calmed down last night that it occurred to me you were in your baseball uniform, which meant you missed the game. It also means you need to bring me your uniform and sweatshirt so that I can get them cleaned. Just bag them up and bring them to me tomorrow and I won't take no for an answer." He was happy to hear her quick laughter.

"Since you put it that way, I'll do it but it's really not necessary. You needed help and that's what friends do – they help when they can. Jeff called last night and reported they might have played better without me since it was our team's first win of the season." This made Cayden laugh since she knew two things – it was their first game and Daniel was probably their best player.

"Well, I won't keep you and I'd better get my act in gear to get ready for church. I'll text as soon as they call about Buddy and thanks ever so much for everything." And with that the call ended but both Cayden and Daniel felt lighter than they had before it had begun.

Not long after, Daniel received the text saying Buddy was doing very well and would be able to come home Monday afternoon. A small paw print emoji followed the message. He thought his day was already getting better and better and he hadn't even arrived at church, where he knew the blessings would keep increasing.

Sunday night, Daniel showed up at Southside halfway through the song service. Aylett Baptist started an hour earlier than Southside and he had hurried north on I-95 to make it in time for Pastor's sermon. He scooted in beside Luke and nodded at Cayden and Allie, who were sitting in the next row and had turned slightly as he sat down. The day had been wonderful right from the beginning, and he just didn't want it to end, which prompted his invitation to treat "the group" to breakfast (or whatever they wanted) at Olaf's. With it being only the four of them, they all piled into his Jeep for the short trip.

Once they were seated and their orders taken, Luke was the first to ask, "So, spill it, man. How'd it go?"

Not waiting to be asked again, Daniel happily filled them in on the entire day, which had unexpectedly included a wonderful Sunday dinner at the head deacon's home. He had enjoyed Mr. Dean's kind offer and the sweet fellowship with his family. After dinner, Mr. Dean gave him a tour of their horse farm located not far outside of Ashland. He had some beautiful horses and had given Daniel an open invitation to stop by for a ride sometime.

"But the highlight of the visit was his Bible collection. It was like a museum, but he allowed me to hold most of them. There were a couple that were too delicate or valuable to be handled. He knew the history of the Bibles and his love for God was evident as he shared his knowledge with me." He finished speaking with a smile and a shake of his head. "That church is blessed to have Mr. Dean."

Not being able to stand it any longer, Cayden blurted out, "So, what did you think of the church? Did you get good vibes? Do you hope they call you as pastor?"

Daniel laughed and answered, "I don't know about good vibes, but I did like the people and the church seems well cared for, which tells a lot about a congregation. As far as hoping they call me as pastor, I'm seriously ready either way. To say it doesn't matter, would sound like I don't care. But it doesn't matter if it's what God's will is for my life and for the people of that church. Funny, but a few years ago I probably wouldn't have felt such calm as I do. If He wants me in Aylett or if He wants me to continue here at Southside for the rest of my days, I'm ready to obey and that's an awesome feeling." As he finished speaking, the others were quiet because none of them had ever been quite that certain of God's leading and it was awesome to see.

They didn't stay long after finishing their meals because the weekend had been emotionally charged for all of them in one way or another. When they arrived back at the church to pick up their cars, Luke prayed a special prayer of guidance for Daniel and healing for Buddy. On the way home, Daniel chuckled to himself thinking how surprised Cayden would have been if she only knew that Luke's prayer for guidance included her future as well as his own.

# Chapter 24

*P*lans for their Memorial Day party were evolving every day. Don and Beth were hosting the shindig with Cayden co-hosting. Her parents, along with Carter and Clarissa were coming and Ila and Phillip would be home in time to join them. Other guests included Allie and her family, Daniel and possibly Mia, Jeff, Teresa and Luke, the Harwell clan, and Paula with her mom, Mrs. Virginia. Ellen had asked if she could bring someone, and they were all excited to see who it would be.

So many of these folks had played a big role in Cayden's last Memorial Day and she couldn't wait to celebrate with them this year. Of course, the party had a patriotic theme, but Cayden had also placed sets of footprints through the yard and on the deck with the real theme for her being "following His lead." She hadn't seen the footprints that day a year ago that led to Don's shop, but they were there; and as she trusted God, He had led her to exactly where He wanted her to be.

As guests arrived late that afternoon, Buddy was the official welcome committee. Cayden told the story that Buddy and a car had done battle and Buddy had war wounds, but you should see the car! Not completely healed, he was content to watch from his comfortable new "playpen" Don had constructed that should hold their little Houdini, at least for the time being. Of course, everyone stopped by often to pet him and sometimes sneak him a treat.

Just about everyone on the guest list had arrived except Ellen and the women were keeping an eye out for her little car. But instead of her red Beetle, she arrived in a gray BMW they all recognized. Her guest was Connor

Murphy! Trying not to be so conspicuous, they all got busy making small adjustments to food tables or just looking in the opposite direction. Ellen had a beau, and it was someone they all approved of and admired. Cayden looked at Beth and both ladies nodded – it was definitely time for a visit to Shamrock Inn to catch up with what was going on in Ellen's world.

Don got everyone's attention and turned it over to Cayden, who quickly thanked each of them for the part they had played over the last year making her feel welcome and at home. Her dad asked the blessing, and the party was on with great food, good music, and the sweetest fellowship. Various games were set up around the property, along with tables and chairs. At dusk, the deck and food tent lights came on. When twinkle lights came on in the many trees around the yard, Cayden gasped with joy, which made Don grin from ear to ear. He had wanted to surprise her, which he'd found difficult to do without her noticing him stringing the lights.

Having Phillip and Ila with them made everything perfect in Cayden's world. As soon as things settled down, the three girls found a quiet spot to catch up and just enjoy each other's company. Talking on the phone and texting was not a substitute for being together and sharing each other's lives. Before too long, they were joined by Phillip, Luke, and Daniel.

Ila spoke up asking Daniel, "So, where is this Mia I've heard so much about? Cayden thought she might come with you."

"Nope, she had other plans for the weekend but sends her apologies," Daniel replied and Cayden thought he looked a little funny as he explained Mia's absence. Come to think of it, he hadn't mentioned Mia lately but that could just be there was nothing new to say.

With that, "the group" with all its original members together again spent time just enjoying each other's company and the easy camaraderie. They were commenting on how nice and quiet it was in this area when fireworks started going off all around them. Quiet was replaced with oohs and ahs as one display after another of sparkling, colorful lights burst into the sky.

Unfortunately, Buddy wasn't a fan of fireworks and Cayden took him inside to enjoy a quieter atmosphere and a little rest thanks to a small pain tablet slipped into a treat. The little guy had enjoyed the day, but rest was just the ticket for him.

The evening ended with special music by anyone who volunteered to play an instrument or sing. Allie and Cayden harmonized on "The Goodness of God" receiving a standing ovation. Not to be outdone, Daniel, Phillip and

Luke sang "God Bless the USA." And on it went until one-by-one people started leaving, noting that the next day was a workday. Cayden's parents were the last to leave, giving their girl big hugs since they were going on home.

Everyone had pitched in to help with cleanup, which prompted Beth to declare the rest could wait until morning. Cayden ran up to check on Buddy and retrieve something she had made for Don and Beth. When she returned, she found them sitting on the deck enjoying the cool breeze and reliving some of the special moments shared throughout the day. Joining them, she relaxed and felt the joys of the day sink in. It had been a wonderful party.

Before long, Don's curiosity got the better of him. "What have you got there, Miss Cayden? A gift from an admirer?"

Laughing at just how close he was to the truth, she played along. "Actually, Mr. Mahoney, it is a gift from an admirer."

Beth was unable to stay out of the fun and piped up with, "An admirer, huh? I can't imagine who it might be from. Can you, Don?"

"Well, there were a few eligible young men here tonight. But which one would be smart enough to give our Cayden a gift?" he replied with a wink.

Cayden suddenly felt sort of funny with the way the conversation was going. None of the guys at the party would be an admirer of hers. Even though they were teasing, she decided to cut the fun short.

"Since you must know, in this instance, I am the admirer giving a gift to two people I admire very much." She rose to hand Beth the package. "I wanted to give you something to let you know how much I love you and appreciate all you've done for me because I can never say *thank you* enough to really express my heart. You've sheltered me, protected me, loved me, mentored me, and shown great compassion to me. But it's hard to buy something for a couple who literally have everything. So, with Carter's help, I made this for you."

Beth was first to gain her voice, "But, Cayden, we've loved every minute of this past year. You bring us such joy. You didn't have to give us anything." Eyeing the gift, she couldn't resist asking, "Can we open it now?"

Cayden nodded and Beth ripped through the wrapping to find a flash drive and a DVD. The DVD was labeled "Don and Beth's Journey" along with the date. They looked at each other and then back at Cayden.

"When I first arrived, one of the things I was awestruck by was Beth's meticulously chronicled photo collection of your life together. I have secretly been borrowing photo albums from your family room over the last six months and scanning the pictures. As I finished one album, I took it back and borrowed another. Carter and I met one Saturday in Richmond for lunch, and I gave him the scanned photos to begin putting together a movie, chronicling your life together thus far," she explained, as she watched understanding dawn on their faces.

"You mean this is a DVD containing my photos? How wonderful!" Beth exclaimed as she jumped up to hug Cayden. "I've thought about having that done but never got around to it. Wow!"

"We took the photos, added some captions and music and now there's a movie. Carter was the technical guru, and we enjoyed spending time working on this for you. Oh, and the flash drive contains the scanned photos," Cayden explained before quietly adding, "There is one thing I think I should tell you before you watch it. In March, after you shared with me about your precious Annie, her baby book was in the family room with the albums. I hope it's all right that I included photos from the baby book in the movie."

When no one spoke, she was sure she had overstepped. It was often hard to discern tears of happiness or tears of sadness or dismay. Their reaction was totally unexpected as they jumped up and headed inside. Not knowing what to do, Cayden just sat still until Don poked his head back out the door and yelled, "Come on, Cayden, we've got a movie to watch!"

The couple sat hand in hand watching their history float by on the screen, starting with their parents and ending with photos from tonight. Unknown to Cayden, Carter had taken shots early in the evening and added them at the end of the movie. The very last photo was of Cayden holding a big sign saying "Thank you! I love you, Beth & Don!! Can't wait to see the sequel."

Laughter, along with oohs and ahs, was the main reaction throughout the movie. When the section including baby Annie started, the music changed to "Jesus Loves Me" and the speed with which the photos changed slowed a bit. Don put his arms around Beth's shoulders as they both smiled through tears. After the movie ended, there were fresh tears as they thanked Cayden for such a special gift and as she again told them how much they meant to her.

The movie had been a success. It was a montage of photos chronicling the lives and loves of two precious people and Cayden was happy they liked it. The next morning, Ellen called her at work to say that Beth had called her first thing and couldn't stop raving about the movie.

She finished her praise with, "You've done a lovely thing for a lovely couple and it's brightened their spirits. I just wanted you to know and to say how thankful I am for you."

After a bit more chit-chat, Cayden couldn't resist asking about Connor. "How did you get it by all of us that you and Connor are an item?"

With a happy sigh, Ellen filled her in. "It's not been easy. The *Feed My Sheep* ministry sort of threw us into each other's paths on a regular basis and next thing I knew he was asking me out to dinner. I accepted on the condition we keep it quiet, just between the two of us, for a while and he agreed. When we go out to eat, we go a little further afield than Fredericksburg and, of course, he's been to the inn for dinner a couple of times."

"Well, we are all over the moon to see you so happy. You two are great together. Beth and I will be by soon so you can fill us in on all the details. But, for now, all I can say is you go girl!"

# Chapter 25

*I*la and Phillip were traveling a great deal of the time, which meant the girls didn't have much time to catch up. But when they did talk it was evident Ila was as happy as any wife could be. She loved her husband, and she loved working alongside him in his ministry. They had decided to renew the lease on Phillip's apartment for six months to have a better handle on scheduling of speaking engagements. It would also give them a chance to think about what it would be like to have no actual home to come back to if they chose to live full-time in an RV.

The good news was they would stay in the Fredericksburg area the week after Memorial Day, which fit in great with Allie and Cayden's schedules. A girls' night was planned for Tuesday and their regular group decided to meet at Olaf's after church Wednesday night. They would leave again Saturday to share the *Feed My Sheep* ministry at a church in Ohio on Sunday. The rest of their time would be used to get their apartment straight with which furniture to keep, unboxing Ila's belongings and everything else that needed to be done to make it their home instead of Phillip's bachelor digs. While Don assured them he didn't mind storing boxes in his garage, they knew that wouldn't be a long-term solution, which meant making it a priority to either make room for those items or get rid of them.

On Tuesday night, the girls met at Cayden's for a lovely lasagna dinner followed with lots and lots of girl talk. When Ila mentioned their plan for sorting and discarding things, Allie came up with the idea of having a yard sale with any proceeds going to the *Feed My Sheep* ministry at Southside. Ila touched base with Phillip, who thought it was a great idea. Before they said good night, plans had been drawn up and a date set for late June. Cayden had cleared it with Beth to have the yard sale at their house and Beth promised to help in any way she could. Allie volunteered to make up fliers to put up around the neighborhood and to post it on Facebook Market. A text was sent to all the *Feed My Sheep* ministry volunteers asking them to contribute items for the sale and all of the replies were positive with Ellen's reply being best of all because she promised to donate baked goods to sell to hungry shoppers. The girls loved it when a plan came together!

Wednesday night after church at Olaf's was a relaxed time with special friends. Luke and Allie were excited that the school year would soon be done. Summer plans were discussed with Allie and Cayden's road trip as a major topic. And, of course, they were all interested to know if Daniel had heard from the church in Aylett yet.

Cayden watched as Daniel's face lit up when he gave them an update. "Mr. Dean, the head deacon, called to say I'm on the short list of candidates." He stopped as they all offered congratulations. "They hope to make the decision soon on their new pastor."

"Are you anxious?" Luke asked. "I know it was nerve racking waiting to hear if I got the teaching job."

"I've been amazed at how calm I am about this. But, as I teach my Sunday school class, I've turned it over to the Lord and am just waiting to follow where He leads me. My heart does do a little happy dance at the thought of being called to Aylett Baptist, but I'll be happy either way." Daniel smiled and gently shook his head as he finished, "It's just awesome knowing God has a plan for me."

Olaf had been happy to see Phillip and Ila and had even sat with the group for a few minutes to catch up on how everyone was doing. Before leaving their table, he asked Phillip if he could hang around for a few minutes before leaving to talk. Feeling prompted by the Holy Spirit, Phillip asked the group to pray for Olaf as they traveled home. Unless he was mistaken, his newly found friend wanted to talk about Jesus.

A short while later, the group called it a night going their separate ways. They had come up with a plan to help the newlyweds work on their apartment over the next two days so it would be at least mostly done before they left for Ohio Saturday morning. So, goodbyes weren't in order just a casual "see you tomorrow after work" was heard as they got into their cars. And as they went their way, each of them prayed for Olaf.

As Olaf watched the others drive away, he joined Phillip at the table. Ila had slipped out with the others and Phillip knew she was in the car bringing him and Olaf to God – him for clarity to speak the Gospel and Olaf to have a receptive heart. For the millionth time, he breathed a breath of thanks for a godly wife.

Olaf was a little uncertain how to start but the conviction behind his questions quickly strengthened his resolve and his voice. "I've been watching you and your small band of friends for a while now and there's something different about you. Several times you've talked to me about Jesus and something you call 'salvation' and I admit I just don't understand. One thing I do know is that you are different, and I want to know how and why." He ended giving Phillip a look which while confused was also determined.

Never without his small New Testament, Phillip pulled it out of his pocket and began to explain just what made him different – Jesus. "You remember me telling you about my years as a homeless man and how someone explained the love of God to me while sharing verses from the Bible?" Olaf nodded and Phillip continued, leading him along what many call the Romans Road, showing him each verse in the Bible.

"First, we all have to admit we have sinned against God as stated in Romans 3:23 *For all have sinned, and come short of the glory of God.* Can you agree to that?" Olaf nodded his head, but his eyes never left Phillip's.

"Okay. There is a penalty for our sin, *For the wages of sin is death*, Romans 6:23. But God loves us so much He doesn't want us to pay that penalty. So, He provided someone to pay it for us – His Son, Jesus Christ. *But God commendeth his love toward us, in that, while we were yet sinners, Christ died for us*, Romans 5:8." Phillip took a minute to let that sink in and was ready when Olaf asked him how that was possible.

"You see, Jesus, God's son, came to earth as a man to live among us and teach us. Though He was man, He was also God and, therefore, could not sin. He chose to be the sinless, innocent sacrifice for the sins of the world – for me and for you. All we must do is believe and ask Him to forgive us of our sins. Here, look at this verse in Romans 10:13 *For whosoever shall call upon the name of the Lord shall be saved.* That means you recognize you're a sinner worthy of punishment, but Jesus took that punishment for you. All you have to do is ask." Again, Phillip waited. This time, Olaf's head was bowed, and Phillip could see tears streaming down his cheeks.

With a broken voice, he whispered, "Can you help me? I want Jesus to forgive me."

"Of course. If you want to accept Jesus' gift of salvation from your sins, you can repeat this simple prayer." Phillip recited the prayer phrase by phrase stopping after each to let Olaf repeat them. "Dear Lord, I know that I'm a sinner and that Jesus died on the cross for me. Please forgive me of my sin, come into my heart and save me. In Jesus' name, Amen."

When Olaf said "Amen" Phillip looked up to find his friend smiling through tears. Both men stood and Olaf grabbed Phillip in a bear hug.

"I've been thinking about this especially since your wedding when the preacher talked about Adam and Eve and sin and then about Jesus and salvation. I even bought a Bible and tried to figure it out, but I just got more confused. But now I see and now I'm saved from my sins!" Even though there were a few folks left in the restaurant, Olaf didn't seem to mind them hearing his testimony or seeing him hugging Phillip enthusiastically. Phillip had seen this many times, but it never grew old. What a mighty and merciful God he served!

Phillip asked Olaf to walk out to the car with him where they found Ila smiling from ear to ear. She quickly admitted she had been watching as she prayed and knew what had just happened. She gave Olaf a hug and told him he would never be the same now that he knew Jesus. Phillip opened the trunk and pulled out a Bible with verses marked that would help a new believer, along with some gospel tracts outlining what Olaf had just experienced.

With one last hug, Phillip and Ila told Olaf good night but not before assuring him they would be in for breakfast the next morning. Olaf waited in the parking lot until they were out of sight before going back in his restaurant. He told his staff to close early for the night as he thanked the last customer. He needed to get home and tell his wife what had happened to him and to use his new Bible to explain it to her too. Remembering what he often heard his small group of friends of Southside say, he said out loud not caring who heard, "God is good all the time and all the time God is good!"

Ila was busily texting the great news to their group when Phillip got in the car. "Well, my dear husband, there's one more soul saved by grace, and we have a new brother in Christ. Have I told you lately how much I love you and how much you love to share the good news with any and every one?" Reaching over she gave him a resounding kiss on the cheek and a pat on the knee. "Can't wait to go in for breakfast tomorrow morning!"

When they arrived at the restaurant for breakfast, the parking lot was almost packed. Not knowing if there would be room for them to sit and enjoy their meal, they decided a to-go bag would work. But, when they walked in the door, Olaf met them and ushered them into the room where they'd had their rehearsal dinner. It was usually open to all customers except during special occasions. As they entered the room, a cheer went up and people they didn't recognize were hugging them.

Seeing their puzzled faces, Olaf explained. "I went home early last night and told my wife and mother-in-law what had happened. Using the Bible and fliers you gave me, I explained and they, too, prayed for Jesus to forgive them. Next thing I knew, they texted our local family and they're here for you to explain about God and Jesus to them too." He finished with a grin and the look of a very happy man.

Phillip looked at Ila and she knew what to do – pray and call their friends. He talked to the group just as he had with Olaf and most of them prayed along with Phillip. By that time, Pastor Harwood, Cayden, Daniel, and about six others from church were there to help as needed. It was a glorious time and just like God to bless in such a miraculous way.

As things quieted down, Olaf announced it was time for breakfast. His staff wheeled in buffet stations for all to enjoy as they celebrated new life in Christ. Pastor Harwood and his team were astonished at what they had witnessed right there in Fredericksburg on a workday in a commercial establishment. God was indeed good, and He had granted them the honor to be a part of something amazing.

The following Sunday Olaf left the restaurant in the hands of his capable staff, which was something he only did on the rare occasion, and joined his family at Southside for worship service. He had bought all of them Bibles and encouraged them to bring them to church Sunday morning. With Phillip in Ohio, Daniel and Luke welcomed Olaf and his family and helped find seats for all fifteen of them. Pastor Harwell's sermon focused on what a new believer should do according to scripture. When he gave the invitation, Olaf led his family to the altar to profess their belief in Christ and to find out how they were to be baptized. Olaf was no longer just a restauranteur – he was a missionary and he had only just begun.

# Chapter 26

Cayden knew she couldn't leave on vacation without spending time with Beth and Ellen and hearing all about Ellen's new romance. She and Beth called the Monday after Memorial Day and invited Ellen over for dinner. At first, they were disappointed to learn that Ellen was expecting one more guest to check in and couldn't leave the inn. Not to be deterred, they offered to bring dinner to her, which she couldn't think of a way to get out of. It wasn't she didn't want to have dinner with her two dear friends. She just didn't know if she wanted to answer all their questions about Connor but then again, she reasoned, it might be fun to let them in on the secret.

As always, the three of them had a ball spending time together, talking and eating. During dinner, the last lodger arrived, and Ellen checked them in before the ladies settled in for a cozy chat in Ellen's private quarters. Dessert and coffee were brought in and set on the table for them to have whenever they were ready but what Beth and Cayden wanted most was to join in Ellen's joy at this new turn of events in her life.

Not one to sit still and wait, Ellen jumped right in with what she called *the beginning of whatever this is*. "You know that Connor has only been at Southside for a couple of years. And, until he retired six months ago, he wasn't always able to attend services because of his duties as chaplain. We met each other the day he joined the church, but our paths didn't seem to cross until *Feed My Sheep* got started. With both of us working in that ministry, we talked regularly just the same as everyone else involved. Then, one night after a planning meeting, he asked if I'd like to go somewhere for coffee.

Dense me thought he wanted to continue talking about ministry concerns or needs and accepted his invitation. Bless him, he never let on that he hadn't invited me out to talk shop, so to speak, but to get to know me. It wasn't until he called me a few days later and was specific that the invitation was of a more personal nature that it occurred to me. We laugh about it now, but it was mortifying at first."

Beth looked at Cayden with a straight face before they both broke out in laughter. How like Ellen that was. She never thought about herself, which was very endearing but could obviously also lead to confusion.

She gave them time to settle down and grab dessert before picking up the story. "He took me to the Irish restaurant in the Nottingham area. You know – the one in the strip mall." When the others nodded their heads, she decided to continue. "Well anyway, imagine me, a true Irish girl who knows how to cook any Irish recipe out there, eating at a place with a leprechaun in the logo!"

This produced another round of laughter because of her earnest expression. Beth couldn't help but ask, "So, did the waiters wear leprechaun costumes?"

Ignoring her friends' mirth, she continued. "I was polite and ate what they considered Irish cuisine. But, as soon as seemed gracious to my host, I invited him to my house the following Friday evening and showed him what *real* Irish food tastes like." Her whole body was almost rigid with agitation to think a man with the name Connor Murphy, of Irish descent, could even think to take *her* to an Irish restaurant.

Cayden tried not to laugh at her borderline indignation but wasn't successful. "I totally understand what you mean but poor Mr. Murphy. He only has a slight Irish accent. Is he from Ireland like you are?"

Ellen gave an almost unladylike sniff before answering. "No, he's not from Ireland but both his parents were. So, he knows decent food. But I guess he's forgotten his mom's special dishes since she's been gone for over forty years and his wife was Italian."

Another round of laughter ensued, and this time Ellen joined in. She had to admit it did sound funny when she said it out loud. "I guess I was lucky he didn't take me to a restaurant specializing in Irish/Italian dishes!" Laughing at her joke, she added, "But he can make a mean pizza."

This time, gales of laughter brought tears to their eyes. Settling in with coffee, Beth brought the discussion around to more recent days. "You've been seeing each other for four months now. What do you think? You seem very comfortable together, and he's certainly a Christian gentleman."

Ellen smiled and her eyes looked a bit starry as she answered. "I'll be honest with you. I never thought there would be another man in my life after Niall died more than twenty years ago. That's a long time to be on my own and forge ahead in life. But Connor makes me smile and laugh. Oh, he can really be a cut-up, which isn't always the way you think of a chaplain."

Unable to resist, Cayden asked if they were dating with a look toward marriage or just for companionship. Ellen's answer surprised her. "We both believe that if a Christian dates someone it should be with the ultimate idea of marriage. So, to answer your question, I have to say we believe this may lead to marriage."

"Are you serious?" Cayden asked. "I've never heard that before. My parents were strict on us only dating a Christian but, I mean, at seventeen who's thinking about marriage?"

Beth chuckled as she replied instead of Ellen. "Don't let Pastor know you haven't heard this before or you'll be getting his sermon on the subject! Just kidding but maybe I shouldn't be about such an important subject. Dating often, if not usually, leads to an intimate relationship that might include holding hands, occasional kisses, etc. If a Christian believes God has a plan for their life and hopes that plan will include marriage, shouldn't those intimate moments be reserved for the one He has for you? To be honest with you, I wasn't sold on the concept until a friend of ours was dating a man who right up front let her know he had no wish to marry. When she described their dates, it saddened me to think she was wasting her time but more importantly her special moments with a man that would never be her husband. That put it in perspective for me. Now, I will say that not many Christians think this way and we surely don't hold it against those who don't. All that to say that it's something each person must decide for themselves."

They could tell Cayden was a bit thrown off guard by the way their conversation had changed course. "It is something to consider and I will. Thinking back on my short relationship with Josh, I can see the logic better. Just because he was attending a Christian college, I took for granted he loved the Lord and I thought we might be building toward something permanent. But look how that turned out. I know I'm sorry for the time and emotions I spent on someone who probably doesn't even know the Lord." Shaking her head, she lightened the mood by asking, "How did we get off on my non-existent love life when we're talking about Ellen and Connor's relationship?"

Noticing the looks that passed between Ellen and Beth with a wink and smile, she continued. "Now, what's that about? There's no man in my life and you know it – unless you count Buddy. Why the sly winks and smiles?"

Ellen chuckled, "So, there's no man in your life? No one that looks at you when he thinks no one notices or drops by unexpectedly?"

"Of course not! Who could there be? I only seem to go to work or church and you know who's there," Cayden countered.

"Exactly! You only go to work or church, and we *do* know who's there." Beth smiled again at Ellen as if to signal a high five was coming.

Wishing the subject had never been brought up, Cayden announced she had to be getting home to let Buddy out. "Glad I drove separately so I wouldn't have to hear more of this stuff on the way home," she said in a joking manner even though she meant every word.

Not to be put off, Beth asked, "Remind me why you drove separately please."

"I had to stop by the church and pick up the bulletin information for Sunday," Cayden replied.

"Well, I decided to run by the grocery store on the way over here and noticed there was only one other car in the church parking lot. Whose was it, Cayden? And since we're discussing it, I'll go one step further and ask why you were still there when I came out of the store," Beth said with a big grin on her face. She was enjoying this way too much.

Sputtering, Cayden stated the car belonged to Daniel, who was there working on his youth meeting message and asked for her opinion. "I would have done the same for anyone. He likes to run things by me sometimes because we're *colleagues*," she stressed.

Ellen held up her hand as if calling a truce. "Okay, honey, you know we're just teasing but there's some truth mixed in with it. Daniel's a very special young man and he's smart too – smart enough to realize how special you are." Before Cayden could say anything else, Ellen gave her a hug and Beth joined in. "We love you Cayden girl and we want God's very best for you. For now, forget what we've said because when the Lord's timing is just right, He'll show you what or who He has for you."

As Cayden gathered up her purse and slipped her shoes on, Ellen packed up some of the left-over dessert for her and Beth to take home. Hoping to end the evening on a lighter note, she said, "Please put extra in my goodie box so I can take some to Daniel tomorrow," for which, she received swats from Beth as she walked out the door.

On the way home, she couldn't get the ideas suggested to her by two precious friends out of her mind. First, the idea of dating only with marriage in mind but more importantly the idea that Daniel might really think she was special.

# Chapter 27

*D*on had hated possibly putting a damper on the girls' plans for a road trip in a sporty convertible. But, when he learned there would now be three passengers and luggage for three females (which to him meant a lot of luggage), he decided to step in and offer his opinion. He took Cayden and Allie to his friend, Byron's, car lot and let them see for themselves that another choice might suit them better for a week on the road. He showed them the car he and his friend thought would better suit them, a silver 2016 Toyota Camry with all the bells and whistles. After a brief discussion of the pros and cons for the best vehicle, they were satisfied that the Camry was the right choice. Byron handed them the keys and they took it for a spin but not before checking out how many cup holders it had, if the seats were comfortable, and if it had Sirius XM. They returned a short while later with happy faces, ready to sign the necessary paperwork. True to his word, Don had gone the extra mile and worked a sweet deal with Byron so that the girls had a safe, sporty, reliable car for a very modest price.

As planned, Marta drove down to Fredericksburg the day before their road trip would begin and spent the night with Cayden. It was fun for the two girls to spend some one-on-one time together. It was like their college days with all the laughter and chatting until well after midnight. Cayden's last conscious thought was a silent prayer of thanks for, well, everything.

Allie arrived at Cayden's bright and early Saturday morning. Don was on hand to make sure they got off okay and to lend a hand if needed. He was pleasantly surprised when the girls embraced him in a group hug with many thanks for his help choosing a car. There was no way all their luggage would fit into the trunk of any of the convertibles they had researched. After all their chatter and giggling subsided, he prayed with them for safe travel and a great time together. Beth and Buddy joined Don as they waved and watched the happy trio start out on their much-anticipated summer road trip.

The girls knew there would be a lot of travel time over the next week and embraced the time as a once-in-a-lifetime chance to bond and grow as not just friends but sisters in Christ. Their itinerary consisted of visits to the Biltmore Estate in North Carolina, Creation Museum and Ark Encounter in Kentucky, and Dollywood in Tennessee. But they had mapped it out so that there was also time to make stops along the way when needed or just to sightsee in a particular area. They were always on the lookout for flea markets or vintage shops. But, on the first day, their emphasis was to just enjoy the trip and their companions. Of course, where to eat was always an interesting debate – so much so that they decided to take turns making the final decision, which had added a fun and sometimes interesting element to their trip.

After only a few stops along the way, they rolled into Asheville early that evening. A few new items were snuggly packed in the trunk thanks to a quick shopping stop in Bristol. Still excited and only slightly road weary, they found a quaint farm-to-table restaurant for dinner (Allie's choice since Marta had chosen where to stop for lunch). After dinner, they strolled through Biltmore Village before checking into their hotel.

Cayden had scoped out a church in Asheville where one of her college professors now pastored for them to attend Sunday morning. Pastor Gregory was happy to see his former student again and equally as glad to welcome them to worship with his congregation. The song service was a wonderful prelude to the uplifting, thought-provoking sermon which followed. As the girls left the church, they were happy to have been in the house of the Lord.

They had tickets to a tour of Biltmore at two o'clock that afternoon, which meant a quick stop at the hotel to change before grabbing a bite to eat. Later, they all agreed the rush had been worth it because touring Biltmore was an eye-opening experience they wouldn't have missed. Cayden, in particular, enjoyed the self-guided audio tour as it directed them along hallways steeped in history stopping at different areas to explain the significance of what she was seeing. Most striking, of course, was the drastic difference between the opulent upstairs and the utilitarian downstairs. The grandeur of the mansion and grounds left the girls speechless but not for long. They talked about different aspects of what they'd seen all that evening and as they traveled to Kentucky the following day.

Thinking aloud, Marta noted, "Seeing all those rich fabrics and fancy ornamentation made my head whirl. But then, I thought of heaven and how nothing on this earth compares to its glory." As the others agreed, she finished up with a happy voice, "And it's ours because we're the Father's children. How cool is that?"

Monday was another travel day with stops along the way. They spent the night in Petersburg where the Creation Museum was located. Cayden had gotten tickets for the museum and the Ark Encounter, which was not quite an hour south. They visited the museum on Tuesday and the Ark on Wednesday absorbing information and mentally readjusting some of their preconceived thoughts as they took it all in.

"I never thought about just how huge the ark actually was!" Allie exclaimed as they pulled into the parking lot. "Just imagine Noah building it following God's instructions and all the while being ridiculed and mocked."

By the time they had meandered through the ark, taking in all the common-sense information presented about how it had to have been built, how much food they would have needed for Noah's family and the animals, and so much more, they marveled at God's providence for anyone who would have entered the ark for salvation. It was such a picture of Jesus and how all anyone must do is to accept His offer of salvation.

"For me, the most exciting and awe-inspiring part is there was only one door to the ark and physical salvation for any who would enter in. When they showed a cross on the door, signifying Jesus is the door to our spiritual salvation, my heart took off singing," Cayden said, as she sighed with contentment. "I love knowing Jesus!"

Later that afternoon, as they traveled to Knoxville where they would spend the night, there were only a few quiet times. Most of the four-hour trip was spent discussing everything they had taken in at the museum and the Ark. One would hardly finish a thought before another chimed in with a comment or a new aspect to consider. They were a very happy kind of tired when they checked into their hotel. It was Cayden's turn to choose dinner and her decision met with sighs of relief and thankfulness. Pizza delivery had never sounded so good.

Dollywood was their destination the following morning. Cayden had purchased their day tickets and knew just where to go when they arrived at the park entrance. While she seemed to be fumbling with her pack looking for the tickets, Allie let out a shriek. Knowing her surprise guest had arrived, Cayden looked up to find Ila hugging the other girls. Phillip had arranged his ministry visits so they would be in the Pigeon Forge area on this particular day and his wife could spend time with her best friends. Cayden had called Ila to let her know where to wait that morning. Having her with them made their group complete and it made riding the rides more fun with four of them. A day that was already going to be great had just ramped up to awesome.

They arrived just as the park opened and stayed until late afternoon. An exhausted group of friends left the park with happy hearts except when they realized Phillip would be picking Ila up shortly and the group would split up.

Ila summed it all up for them. "This has been the best fun. Just being with you three has been wonderful but getting to act like teenagers on the rides has been a blast."

She had let Phillip know when to pick her up and was giving them all hugs when he arrived. Seeing tears in their eyes, he suggested something he was sure they would like. "Here's a thought. The pastor I met with today has set up meetings tomorrow with two other pastors in the area. Sorry, honey, but it looks like you'll be on your own tomorrow." Then he grinned and clicked his fingers. "But wait a minute. Didn't you say the girls were going to spend a second day in Gatlinburg? Do you think they might take pity on my sweet wife and let her hang out with them tomorrow?"

Before he finished speaking, all four girls were squealing and talking over each other in their excitement. Ila just grabbed her husband and gave him a sound kiss along with a quick "Yes!" And, so, plans were made for him to drop Ila off at their hotel the following morning.

Cayden punched Phillip in the arm and smiled up at him. "You rascal, that's such a cool idea. We'll take good care of her but don't forget to give her your wallet or at least your credit card!"

The decision for dinner that night had been made as a group. Marta and Allie had never eaten at Dixie Stampede, but Cayden had eaten at the restaurant in Myrtle Beach. They were entertained while eating good food and unwinding from a terrifically memorable day of fun and friends.

Friday was filled with shopping, eating, and laughing with a *shampoo, rinse and repeat* mentality. The Camry's trunk was almost to the point of not closing by the time they dropped Ila off at her hotel. Plenty of hugs and tears marked the end of a great day with promises of phone calls to keep in touch following Ila into the lobby.

A light dinner was all anyone wanted after the day they'd had, and all agreed salads would be just the thing. After a quick trip through Chic-fil-A's drive-through, the hotel was their last stop for the day. A quiet, relaxing evening was just what they needed, along with getting their things ready for an early start for home the next morning.

Cayden was surprised when shortly after she'd finished her salad her phone rang and she saw it was Daniel calling. The girls had kept their families and some of their friends up to date on their trip with texts, photos or calls but she hadn't included him. Before her conversation with Beth and Ellen, she probably would have been communicating tidbits of their travels with Daniel but the things they had said left her wondering just what her relationship with him was. So, it was interesting to have him calling.

She excused herself and went out into the hall before answering. "Hey Daniel! How are you?" Man, she thought, what a great conversationalist I am.

"Hi Cayden. I'm well. How are things going on your girls' road trip? I heard Beth and Ellen talking Wednesday night and it sounds like you're having a great time." Daniel, at least, sounded normal.

Okay, this was going to be easy, just like always, Cayden thought. "Oh, we are! We've had a blast but we're ready to come home tomorrow. Guess what – Ila joined us at Dollywood yesterday and then spent today with us too. They were in the area meeting with pastors and Phillip was kind enough to let us borrow her." Now, she thought, I sound like a rambling idiot.

Daniel chuckled, "I guess if you gave her back that's what matters. Do you have a minute? There's something I wanted to tell you."

Without hesitation, she said, "Of course. Nothing's wrong, is it? You sound so serious." And suddenly, there were butterflies or possibly bees, flying around her stomach.

"Everything's fine. In fact, I'm calling with good, no make that great, news. Aylett Baptist has asked me to be their full-time pastor. Mr. Dean called this morning, and I took until just a few minutes ago to pray and make sure this was God's leading. Just got off the phone with him accepting the offer." He abruptly stopped, took a deep breath and said, "Cayden, that means I'm a pastor. Oh, my goodness!"

All of Cayden's butterflies disappeared. This was Daniel, her Daniel, and he had just received confirmation from God that he was to pastor the flock at Aylett Baptist. Excitement built in her heart and in her voice. "Oh, Daniel! That's fantastic! While I'm not surprised they chose you, I know what it must mean to be certain of God's calling and His desire for your life. Congratulations!!"

"Thanks, Cayden! I guess I better call my folks and tell them and Pastor Harwell too," he said still with excitement shining through his voice.

"You mean you haven't told them yet?" was all she could think of saying. Her brain was shouting other things, but her mouth could only ask that one question. She realized she was holding her breath.

"Yes, without even thinking I called you first." As if realizing how that might sound, he quickly added, "But then again alphabetically you're right near the top of my contact favorites list. Well, I better go. See you Sunday morning." And with that he was gone.

Cayden sat in the hotel lobby for a few minutes to collect her thoughts. This was big news. Soon there would be no Daniel whistling as he walked into the office each morning and no Daniel leading singing during services or leading the youth class. She walked back in their room in a daze.

"Where did you go? We were about to..." Allie stopped mid-sentence. "Are you okay, Cayden? Is something wrong back home? You look like you've seen a ghost." She guided Cayden to the couch and motioned Marta to join them.

"Come on, Cayden, you're scaring us. Was it your Beth or one of our moms?" Marta asked with her voice rising in pitch.

"No, nothing's wrong," she finally was able to say trying to sound lighthearted. "It was Daniel. He's been offered the pastor position at Aylett Baptist and just wanted me to know."

Marta and Allie looked at each other with questions in their eyes. Cayden took things in stride. Why would such good news for their friend make her look like a family member had died? And then, it hit them. Cayden had finally realized what so many of them had known for quite a while. She and Daniel weren't just friends. They weren't sure what the actual term for their relationship was, but Daniel and Cayden were more than friends and they had been wondering just when Cayden would see it. Obviously, the time was now.

# Chapter 28

The trip home on Saturday was eventless and a bit quieter than the beginning of their journey a week earlier. All of them were exhausted, and they were ready to be home. The seven-hour trip would seem even longer if they couldn't figure out how to talk with Cayden about Daniel. They had tried the night before, but she said there was nothing to discuss and went about her nightly routine.

Marta had brought up Daniel's good news at breakfast, but Cayden just smiled. Allie tried a little later to draw Cayden out of herself, but she assured them she was fine. When she offered to drive, Allie quickly jumped in the driver's seat before Cayden could. In her current frame of mind, driving a long distance was the last thing she, or they, needed.

A stop for gas seemed the perfect time to get to the bottom of just what was bothering their friend so much that she had hardly spoken a word for three hours. After everyone made a quick trip inside to take care of necessities and stock up on snacks, Allie jumped in feet first.

"All right, we're ready for the last leg of our wonderful road trip. We're about four hours from home but we are not leaving this parking lot until we've restored peace in all our hearts." She stopped to see how Cayden, who was now riding shotgun, reacted to her declaration. At first, she thought Cayden hadn't heard because she continued staring out the window but then Allie saw the tears rolling down her cheeks and could see her chin quivering.

Sensing her friend's despair, Marta began praying out loud. "Dear Lord, our precious girl is hurting, and we don't know how to help. You know what's going on and you are really the only one who can comfort her but please help

Allie and me to know how to minister to Cayden right now, here in this rental car, hours from home. Help us to love her through whatever is hurting her and to be the best sisters we can be for her."

When she finished praying, all three girls were in tears, but a new peace seemed to have settled on them. Cayden, who had been openly sobbing, was calmer as her two friends waited for a cue to what they should do next.

"I'm sorry to be a wet blanket," she said with a slight smile as she wiped tears from her face. "No pun intended." The others laughed, encouraged that she could make a little joke.

"Even though I prayed God would lead Daniel in the decision of being pastor at another church, I hadn't thought what that would really be like. I mean even though sometimes he's been like a pesky brother; he's also been a constant in my life this past year and I've gotten used to him at work, at church, and recently even in my private life. When he called last night, I realized how much I would miss him, and it floored me. That's why I've not been able to discuss it even with my best friends. To put it plain and simple, I'm confused," she confessed, finally able to raise her head and look at Allie. "He called me before he called anyone else with the good news."

Allie and Marta both gasped at this bit of news because it was surprising even to them that Daniel hadn't called his parents, Pastor, or even Luke first. Cayden saw them smile at each other sort of the way Ellen and Beth had at dinner that night. It appeared she was missing something, and she needed to know what that something was.

"Okay, since you want to talk, explain the smiles you just exchanged. Ellen and Beth have been doing that too and I want in on the secret." Cayden's voice was stronger, and the tears had stopped flowing. "What do you know that I don't?"

Allie and Marta exchanged another look and Marta gave a nod. Allie took a few seconds before replying to Cayden's question. "For a while now, those of us who know you well and love you so much have noticed a shift in your relationship with Daniel. Yes, at first, you saw him the same way I do as just another brother to put up with his shenanigans. That was easy to understand because you know what a pesky brother looks like."

Marta took over at this point. "Even long distance with only texts and phone calls, I felt the gradual change. I chalked it up to you just getting used to each other and accepting his flaws and quirks. But something seemed to shift a little after Thanksgiving and a little more after your Sunday school class Christmas party."

Cayden was really shocked at this. "The Christmas party? Josh came with me to that party, and I hardly spent any time with Daniel. What did you notice in me after the party?"

Allie joined in with her observations. "Well, for me, it wasn't you but Daniel. When you walked in Jeff's living room with Josh, Daniel looked like he'd been punched in the gut. Ila noticed it too."

"I guess he did act a bit odd when he asked me about Josh the following Monday morning," Cayden admitted.

"You mean the same morning it snowed, and he just magically appeared to make sure you got to work safely?" Allie interjected with an obvious wink. "But all those things were just the beginning inklings as to what we were seeing happen. When you found Buddy and Daniel helped you, what Ila and I had noticed earlier but filed away in the back of our minds started to emerge as a definite difference in how you related to each other. Then, Buddy went missing and even you admitted Daniel was the first person you thought to call and that he had even missed a baseball game to help you. Right?"

Marta summed it up easily, "Those of us who know and love you have had a front row seat to watching what all of us agree to be the beginnings of a sweet romance. And, before you ask, yes, I talk with Allie and Ila, and this has been the main topic of conversation."

Cayden had stopped crying, and a small smile was playing around the corners of her mouth. "You mean you think Daniel might think I'm special?" When the other girls nodded, she continued. "Beth and Ellen said the same thing the other day. I'd decided to tuck it away and ponder it after we got back from our road trip, and it worked pretty well until last night."

Allie noticed a shadow fall across Cayden's face just thinking about Daniel's call and decided it was time to put this topic to bed – for now. "Cayden, here's my advice and I believe Marta will agree. We have four hours left before our wonderful road trip is history. You are a planner, a thinker, and you need time to mull over everything we've shared with you and any memories and emotions involved. So, try to put it in the back of your mind as a sweet task to be done when you get home and have some alone time with God and a chance to put things in perspective. Do you think you can do that, or do we need to call Ila? You know Phillip would rent her a car and send her to us just like that," she finished with a snap of her fingers.

This made Cayden laugh, which was music to her friends' ears. "You're right. I do need to pray coherently about what's been flying around in my head and heart. Sorry if I've ruined our last day together."

Pulling up the large bag of snacks, Marta exclaimed, "How can any day be ruined when we're together and we have these yummy snacks – all of which must be eaten before we reach Fredericksburg because, as everyone knows, what happens on a girls' road trip stays on the road trip!" She threw candy bars and gummy bears in Cayden's direction, which brought on another laugh.

"Okay, you win. But, if you don't mind, I'd like to catch a catnap. After not sleeping much last night and my crying jags, I'm exhausted." And, with that, she and Marta changed seats, so she was in the back where she had the whole seat to try and get as comfortable as the seatbelt allowed. "You don't know how much you mean to me and thank you for being honest with me. I know I'll have lots of questions later but, for now, I feel much, much better."

Allie and Marta chatted and sang along to music on the radio as they counted off the miles between them and home. The plan was for Marta to spend the night with Cayden and travel home after Sunday school the next morning. When she realized their projected arrival time was mid-afternoon, she decided she would take a quick break and head on home instead. While the past week had been better than she had even imagined, it was time for her to sleep in her own bed and, more importantly, to see Wade.

Three tired but happy girls climbed out of the car and were greeted by Beth and a very excited Buddy. Cayden scooped him up into her arms enjoying the affection he so easily showed her. Luggage and packages were divided up between cars as they all tried to fill Beth in on their adventures.

After holding up her hands in surrender, Beth suggested further discussion wait until tomorrow night after church. She would even provide the pizza and promised to Facetime Marta in so that she could be a part of the fun. They agreed and hugs, with a few tears, were shared before Marta pointed her car north and Allie headed south. Beth and Buddy helped Cayden take her luggage and shopping bags up to her apartment. With a quick hug and a "glad you're home," Beth left Cayden to unpack and relax.

"Buddy, you and I have a lot of talking to do but, for now, I just want to unpack, take a nice long shower, and put my feet up," she said wile rubbing his head the way he liked. When he whined and looked up into her eyes, she added, "Of course you can relax with me and just wait until I show you what I bought for you while I was away."

After she and Buddy were happily ensconced on the sofa, she felt ready to really think about what the last twenty-four hours had revealed to her. First though, she knew it was time to take it all to the Lord and ask for His guidance and comfort. Afterwards, she replayed her conversations with Daniel, Allie, and Marta trying to piece together, with God's help, just what was happening. Surprisingly, tears and sadness were not the result of those thoughts. Instead, she felt awed by the real possibility that she and Daniel might be at least falling in "like."

# Chapter 29

Cayden was looking forward to Sunday morning and getting back into her routine and, of course, being a part of church services. She wasn't sure how she would react when she saw Daniel, but she knew the Lord would be leading her in the way He wanted her to go. One thing she did know was that she would properly congratulate him, with no reservations, on his appointment as pastor at Aylett Baptist.

The first thing she did upon arriving early for Sunday school was check to see if there was anything she needed to take care of before services started. Finding everything just as it should be, she was getting ready to open the office door when Daniel walked in.

When he saw her, his face lit up with a big smile as he welcomed her back. "We've missed you around here. I didn't have anyone to pick on and Pastor just doesn't care for me using him as a substitute."

Noticing that Daniel didn't seem ill at ease or uncomfortable with her, she relaxed and greeted him as usual. "Well, I guess it's a good thing I'm back so that your last days at Southside aren't in the doghouse with Pastor. This place won't be the same without you, but I hope you know how truly happy I am for you." She hesitated just a moment before giving him a quick hug and opening the office door. "Oh yeah, you definitely need to remind me to instruct you on the best way to meet your new secretary and what *not* to do." She heard him chuckling as the door closed and her world seemed to be upright again.

Jeff welcomed Allie and Cayden back and they gave a quick overview of their week, including their time with Ila and Phillip. When Jeff asked how they liked Ark Encounter, Allie was happy to give a glowing report and assure everyone it was worth the trip.

Cayden was happy to see Olaf and many of his family members in the worship service. Many of those who had accepted Christ had been baptized the previous Sunday morning. It was a true picture of God's amazing grace to look at them and see how God's hand had worked so that Olaf would ask Phillip about Jesus, which led to Olaf sharing his new faith with his family. When Daniel began the song service, Cayden sang with love, praise, and thanksgiving. God was, indeed, good to them and to her in particular.

When Beth had invited Allie and Cayden to come over after church Sunday night and tell them all about their travels, the girls had no idea how many others would also be invited. It was such fun to relive their adventures with the people she loved so dearly. As promised, Marta and Wade joined on Facetime. Looking around the room, Cayden thanked God yet again for leading her to this place, to live among these people, and to be loved by them.

Trip stories and pizza with lots of other food went on for quite a while. Eventually, Pastor reminded them that they'd better leave so that his secretary could get a good night's sleep before reporting back to work the next morning. Amid hugs and laughter, everyone went their separate ways and Cayden went home to Buddy. The travel and adventures were great but being back home was awesome.

She met with Pastor and Daniel first thing Monday morning to discuss what plans were in place for hiring a new youth pastor. The deacons had met Saturday and agreed with Pastor's recommendation to begin by contacting some of his fellow pastors and a few professors he knew well to see if any of them knew young men who would be good candidates. He had drafted a letter, which Cayden would type and send by overnight mail. In the meantime, Daniel would begin making a notebook like the one Gail had created for the secretarial position outlining his duties and other helpful information.

The day flew by, and Cayden found herself happy to be back into the groove of her everyday life. She kept the idea of what the office would be like when Daniel left them at bay by remembering to enjoy each day instead of borrowing from tomorrow. By the time she left for the day, the letters had been overnighted and she had a good handle on any tasks she had left over from her week away.

Beth called as she was driving home and invited her to come over for supper. Don was going to grill, and she was fixing up some summery dishes to enjoy on a hot June evening. Her offer to bring dessert was met with news that thrilled her heart – Beth was making her famous strawberry shortcake. Unsure what the ingredients were that set Beth's dish above all others, Cayden only knew she could eat a bucket of the stuff.

Don and Beth had outdone themselves with the delicious meal, which she recognized had been tailored specifically to her because all the dishes were her self-proclaimed favorites. Afterwards, they sat on the shaded deck enjoying the breezes and watching the appearance of fireflies as the day waned into dusk. Conversation rose and fell as the quiet evening wrapped itself around them – that is until Don announced he was going in to watch the Braves "whoop up on the Red Sox," which meant he was going to watch a baseball game on his huge flat screen.

Beth broke the quiet with a simple question, "Cayden, is everything okay?"

Surprised, Cayden took a second before answering. "Yeah, things are okay. I couldn't have said that Friday night or Saturday but I'm all right."

"You know you can't just say something like that and expect me to leave it alone," Beth teased. "I noticed something amiss when you girls got home Saturday but didn't want to pry. Then, your mom called."

"Wait – my mom called you?" Cayden shouldn't have been caught off guard at Beth's comment since she knew her mom and Beth had become good friends and talked occasionally.

Beth took a sip of tea and settled back in her chair so she could see Cayden's face better. "She's concerned that something happened on the road trip and asked if I'd picked up on anything. Her first thought was that maybe being together for a solid week might have stressed your relationship with the girls, but I assured her you girls seemed fine when you got home." Seeing no distress or tears on Cayden's face, she continued. "Ruling that out, I began to wonder if the conversation Ellen and I had with you before you left had caused a problem."

"No, it really didn't. Yes, it made me think but, as I told Allie and Marta, I was pretty much able to park those thoughts until I got back home so that it wouldn't spoil our trip. That is until Friday night." Cayden replied with a quick squeeze of Beth's hand.

"Don't keep me in suspense. What changed Friday night?" Beth asked even as realization dawned in her mind. "Daniel got the call to pastor at Aylett Baptist Friday night. Did that have anything to do with it?"

155

Laughing lightly at Beth's intuitive nature, she simply said, "Yes." Getting up to walk around the deck and check on Buddy, who was happily snoozing in his playpen, she elaborated. "He called Friday right after we returned to our hotel room and his news threw me for a loop. I'd been praying for him to get the call if that's what God's will is for his life, but I'd never given one thought to how that would actually be. I mean no Daniel in my life hadn't crossed my mind until it slammed me in the heart."

Beth moved closer and put her arm around the younger woman's shoulders. "Ellen called me as soon as she heard Daniel's good news and suggested we might call to let you know. She obviously had realized what it would mean to you once you examined it. But, after praying together about it, we knew it wasn't our place. Our place was to pray for you and for Daniel, which we have been doing overtime."

"Thank you for praying because I pretty much shut down on Allie and Marta until a few hours into our trip home. When we stopped for gas, they announced we weren't going any further until I let them know what was going on." Cayden could smile about it now. But, at the time, it hadn't struck her as funny. "For almost an hour we sat in the car praying, talking, and eventually eating. They were as honest as you and Ellen were with me concerning Daniel and Allie had the good judgment to suggest I try to put it away until I was alone at home to examine just what was going on in my head and heart. Feeling better and realizing she was right, I asked if they minded me sleeping in the backseat. Next thing I knew, we were pulling into your driveway."

"God's given you some very special young ladies as friends. Too bad Ila hadn't been around. I can hear her very matter-of-factly telling you what was what and then giving you a big bear hug." Beth grinned at the mental image of Ila on her high horse, determined to fix what was broken.

Laughing out loud, Cayden told her how Allie had threatened to call Ila, who would undoubtedly rent a car and meet up with them to do just that. She let Beth know how she had spent the remainder of Saturday praying and looking at the situation.

"I noticed you seemed better last night and that you and Daniel weren't uncomfortable with each other. In fact, I'd decided that I was wrong about what must have been the problem. Obviously, God really worked in your heart." Looking at her sweet "adopted daughter," she saw that Cayden was back on track. She knew that didn't mean this thing with Daniel and his leaving Southside would be easy, but she felt comfortable Cayden would handle it with grace. "That leaves one question and I'm happy with whatever your answer is."

"What's the question? Bring it on," Cayden answered with a tilt of her head and an inquisitive look.

"Do I call your mom and fill her in or do you?" Beth grinned as she stood up to take in their dessert dishes. "She knows I was going to talk with you and is expecting a call from one of us."

Cayden stood too and started to help do the final dinner cleanup before Beth shooed her away. "Since you're so stubborn and won't let me help, I guess it'll be me," she said with mock surrender as she hugged her friend. "Thank you, Beth, for everything but especially for loving me!"

A call to her mom had been just what she needed to finally feel back to her usual self. After teasing her about having Beth as a secret agent to keep track of her, they quickly buckled down to the real reason for her call. Cayden went to bed late but had the best night's sleep in over a week.

# Chapter 30

Pastor Harwell's letters had resulted in some great candidates for Southside's new youth pastor. He did a telephone interview with several of them before setting up appointments for three to meet with him and the deacons. This kept Cayden busy with scheduling the meetings and making any necessary travel arrangements, such as flights, rental cars, and hotel rooms. By the end of the first week, two candidates had been interviewed and the final candidate would arrive Monday morning. Pastor hoped the process would be complete early the second week so that Daniel could spend as much time as possible with his replacement.

Daniel was working hard on making comprehensive notes so that his successor would know, at least on paper, about each of the kids in Southside's youth group. Glad it was summer and school was out, he was trying to spend some time with each of them. As happy and excited as he was to become pastor of a church, his heart broke each time he did what the kids called his "farewell tour." Knowing Pastor would follow God's leading in the selection of the new youth pastor made his present circumstances easier.

The final candidate came with glowing references. Simon Peter Walker (a name that Cayden knew would give the kids a chuckle) was a 6'3" black man with the build of a linebacker. He grew up in Richmond and returned there after receiving a Bachelor of Arts degree in Bible with Youth Ministries concentration from Pensacola Christian College. His current job was that of guidance counsellor at a public middle school.

After Pastor and the deacons met with Simon, they asked him to wait in the sanctuary. Cayden was surprised because the other candidates had been thanked with a promise that they would be hearing something shortly. Next, Pastor asked her to have Daniel join him and the deacons. About ten minutes later, she was asked to also join the group where they asked for her observations and opinion of Simon during the planning stages of the interview and while interacting with him that morning. She was pleasantly surprised when Pastor announced that Simon was their candidate of choice. All that was left was to offer him the position.

Cayden ushered Simon back into the meeting room and was asked to stay. Pastor advised Simon that they were all in agreement he was the man God would have them offer the job of youth pastor to. He outlined the salary and other pertinent employment information before asking Simon if he needed time to consider or to discuss it with his wife.

"No sir. Coral and I have been praying since your first call and we both feel comfortable this is where God would have me, that is us, serve. Just now, in the sanctuary, with only God and me, He further solidified that knowledge," Simon answered. He hesitated before adding, "There is one thing I think you should know that I didn't want you to be aware of in case it would hold any sway over your decision."

You could have heard a pin drop the room had grown so quiet. When he finished with "My older sister is Amy Hawkins," laughter erupted around the table. Don, as head deacon, was the first to stop laughing and speak. "Well, if that's all that might sway us or you, there's no problem! We love Amy, Landon and their children. You really had us going!"

"Now that's out of the way, I accept and just need to know when you would like me to start. I'm not working this summer and can start anytime," Simon reported, much to the joy of everyone in the room.

It was decided he would join Southside as youth pastor on Wednesday and be introduced to the congregation, and more importantly to the youth group, that night. Daniel's replacement had been hired and in less than a week he would no longer be a part of Southside Baptist's staff or membership. He had mixed emotions for just a minute before rejoicing over what was to come and for God's leading Simon to care of his youth group.

Earlier in the year, Daniel had planned a trip with the teens to Skyline Drive to hike down to Dark Hollow Falls. He couldn't help but shake his head in wonder as he realized God's hand in the timing of the trip – the last Saturday of his time at Southside. No matter how many times he saw obvious signs of God's leading, he still marveled that the creator of the universe loved him, cared for him, and moved in his life. He chuckled as he said out loud, "I know what Cayden would say. 'God is good all the time and all the time God is good!' And to that, I add Amen and Amen!!"

A group of twenty-three set out from the church at eight o'clock on a warm Saturday morning for the two-hour ride to the Dark Hollow Falls trailhead. Although the almost two-mile hike wasn't considered difficult, it was steep and rocky, but the sights along the route and the falls themselves would be worth the trip. As a sort of symbolic passing of the torch, Daniel would lead the group down to the falls and Simon would lead them back up. Both men thought it was a bit corny but also quite meaningful, which they liked.

Daniel had asked Ellen and Connor to take charge of setting up lunch at one o'clock at Big Meadows picnic area. They had recruited Don and Beth to help and to be a part of the fun. Don was sure the right term would be "adventure" because invariably when you took a bunch of teens into the wild, there would indeed be some type of drama. He had packed their large first aid kit, along with bug repellant and sun block for the just-in-case of life.

Before the hikers took off down an unknown mountain trail, Daniel reminded them to be aware of the rocky terrain, critters in general but especially bears and snakes, and poison oak. Several of the timid teens asked questions, which he answered truthfully but tactfully, and which prompted him to have everyone buddy up into pairs for the hike. A last call was made for anyone wanting sun block or bug repellant before Daniel led them in prayer and they were off into the wild.

Cayden paired up with a rather shy girl who was relatively new to their youth group. Sarah and her family had only recently moved to Fredericksburg, and she was still trying to find her footing in a new place and a new church. While the church teens were good kids and for the most part friendly, they could forget what it was like to feel alone even in a large group. Watching them choose buddies, Cayden decided it might be nice to save Sarah the anxiety of possibly not being chosen and asked her quickly if she would mind walking with her. The smile on Sarah's face let her know she'd done the right thing.

"Thanks, Ms. Cayden, I don't really know anyone very well yet. But I am determined to get to know the kids better today. This summer before my senior year is important and I want to enjoy it with friends. My mom reminded me that to make friends I have to be friendly and that's what my plan is." Sarah was so earnest when she spoke it almost made Cayden laugh but instead, she smiled and told her that her own mother had reminded her of that very thing only a few months ago.

"And you know what? It worked. I've only been in Fredericksburg for a year and look at all the wonderful friends I've made. But it wasn't always easy being the new kid on the block." Remembering back to a few lonely days last summer made Cayden even more thankful for her mom's advice. "Tell you what, I'll join you in prayer as you settle into your new life here that God will bless you with a ton of new friends and that this summer will be your best ever."

After that, their conversation wandered over lots of topics making them realize how much they were alike. They both liked to sing and kayak, and Sarah was thinking about attending Liberty University. College selection and classes pretty much dominated the remainder of the trip down to the falls. Once everyone had arrived, Cayden introduced Sarah to a couple of the girls who were also contemplating Liberty as their college of choice. Later, when Simon announced they were going to head back up for lunch, Sarah asked if Cayden would mind if she walked with Corrin, who had all sorts of intel to share about, well, everything. Happy to see the girl settling in, she quickly assured her that would be fine and watched her almost skip back to her new friend.

Daniel was bringing up the rear of the group when he noticed Cayden was walking alone. "Didn't I tell everyone to buddy up? Where's your partner, young lady?" he asked with mock severity.

Trying not to laugh, she answered very woefully, explaining how her partner had thrown her over for another more interesting candidate. Seeing as how they were now at the very end of the group, he invited her to be his partner for the return hike, which worked out well because his buddy had also abandoned him for someone else. In unison, they said "Kids!"

"So, how does it feel turning over your youth group to Simon?" Cayden wondered out loud. "Can't be easy after four years watching them grow up to just leave them even in very competent, caring hands."

Daniel slowly shook his head before replying. "It's not easy, but yet it's not hard either because I know this is what God has planned not just for me but for the kids. Simon is going to be great with them and for them. I wish you had been in the youth group meeting Wednesday night. He asked if he could give the devotion and it was exactly the right balance of scripture, knowledge sharing, and putting them at ease with the new guy. The ability to do that can't be learned, it's a God-given talent."

"You have that too, you know," Cayden reminded him. "I've watched you over the last year with all the children, not just the teens and they not only like you, but they also trust you. That's huge and I believe it will be a major asset as you settle in as pastor at Aylett Baptist because you have that type of rapport with adults also."

Daniel excused himself for a moment to remind some of the boys to stay on the path and to stop pestering the girls. "Sorry about that. Those guys love to push boundaries, but they listen when I talk to them, which is a huge blessing." He paused for just a second before picking back up on their previous conversation. "It's nice of you to say that about how I interact with adults because I have wondered if the majority of my experience being with youth might leave me with a big learning curve when dealing mainly with adults – switching tracks, so to speak."

Without hesitation, Cayden answered with conviction. "Truthfully, I believe your background with children gives you a big advantage as you begin pastoring a church. Some pastors have no idea how to relate to children. Your work as youth pastor has not just been dealing with children; in fact, a very large part of what you do depends on your relationship with the parents. And the parents at Southside are sorry to see you go while at the same time they're happy with the path God has chosen for you. Never doubt that, Daniel, and, more importantly, rest assured that God would only lead you to a place where He can use you to bless His people."

"Well, I wasn't fishing for compliments, but I sure do appreciate your candid observations. All kidding aside, Cayden, your opinion really means a lot to me." As he finished that sentence, a shriek from just ahead had him sprinting uphill to see what the commotion was all about. She didn't mind the interruption because she needed a minute to mull over what he'd said and to calm her heart after finding out he considered what she thought was important to him.

Returning to her side, he said with a big grin, "No problem. One of the girls saw a little black snake, which has proven to be a real motivator for this group to move a little quicker back to the top." But that had effectively brought their easy conversation to an end. For the rest of the return trip, they chatted about some office things or about Buddy.

By the time they'd reached the picnic grounds, tales of the snake sighting had grown especially in the girl ranks. A few scraped knees and hands from falls were attended to while Don reminded them all to check for ticks. This brought on another onslaught of squeals and not just from the girls. Beth joined Don as chief inspectors when a teen thought there might be a tick on them. A head count verified everyone had returned safely and lunch was served shortly thereafter.

Ellen and Connor had outdone themselves with grilled hamburgers and hotdogs and all the trimmings. The hike had stoked appetites, and everyone ate heartily. Games were planned for after lunch until the group would leave for the return trip back to church. Children played or sat around talking while adults packed up everything and then plopped down in lawn chairs for a much-deserved rest.

Phillip and Ila had driven up for lunch in Daniel's Jeep and would ride back on the bus. Daniel had asked them to do this so that he could leave right after lunch. Sunday was going to be a big day for him, and he wanted to be rested and prepared for his first day as pastor. As he loaded up his gear, Simon called the group together for prayer with Daniel and a big group hug. Cayden wasn't the only one openly crying as they watched him drive away but she was the only one whose heart seemed to be breaking.

Sensing their friend's sadness, Allie and Ila asked her to join them for a stroll around the picnic grounds. Ila assured them that Phillip would help keep an eye on the teens while they were gone as the three best friends walked and talked.

"I keep thinking back to the first time I met Daniel and the whole coffee/candy bar fiasco and realize how far we've come in our friendship," Cayden said with a sad smile. "The office will not be the same without him that's for sure."

Ila grinned at Allie and used air quotes as she said, "Friendship?"

Cayden stopped and looked surprised. "Why the air quotes? Daniel and I have a nice friendship."

"Of course you do," Allie said trying to keep the conversation calm. Ila could sometimes jump in where angels feared to trod with the result being less than hoped for. "Ila just meant to question if that's all you think you have with Daniel – friendship. I mean he and I are friends and I'll miss him but not quite as much as it seems you will."

"Well, duh! I work with him. You only go to church with him, and we all occasionally hang out together. But it makes sense that I may miss him a bit more because of our work relationship." The other girls could see that even Cayden wasn't buying what she was saying, which blessedly caused them all to start laughing and lightened the mood. They were still laughing when they heard the bus horn signal it was time to leave.

# Chapter 31

Simon and Coral had decided to look for a place to live in Fredericksburg instead of commuting from Richmond. When Coral asked Cayden if she would mind helping her find an apartment or townhouse, Cayden was only too happy to help. In addition to giving her a chance to get to know Coral, it also helped occupy her thoughts.

The couple often spent nights in the church's prophet's chamber, which made it easier to look for a new home. Allie also joined them on some of their visits to prospective homes and the three of them always had fun. Although it only took a month to find the right place, that was plenty of time for the girls to become fast friends.

Moving day was a time of great fun as so many volunteered to help pack and move their new youth pastor and his wife out of their old apartment into their new home. Cayden wasn't surprised when Daniel showed up for moving day but seeing him did funny things to her heart. He was the same old Daniel, joking and teasing but there seemed to be a new air of maturity about him that she supposed came with the responsibilities of a pastor. She decided it suited him.

Simon had settled in and was doing a wonderful job. Cayden helped in any way she could to make sure he felt comfortable in his new position and in a new place. But the office just wasn't the same without Daniel.

A phone call from her mom brightened her mood. She was going home for the weekend and the thought of getting away for a few days was just what she needed. In fact, she asked Pastor if it would be okay for her to take Friday off to make it a longer weekend and he agreed and even told her to take

Monday off too. He wouldn't be in the office, but Simon could hold things down. So, her weekend turned into four days in which to regroup and hopefully get her heart under control.

Thursday after work, she set off for another road trip but this time with Buddy as her companion. He was great company in his little car seat. He listened to her chatter and share her thoughts and heart with him without even once interrupting; and when he got tired, he simply closed his eyes and dozed off. As they sped south, her spirits lifted in anticipation of time with her family and especially with her mother.

Friday morning was glorious. After an early family breakfast, Cayden's dad and brother set out for work leaving her and her mom to relax over a second cup of coffee before starting their day. They hadn't even discussed plans for the day or even the rest of the weekend and that was just fine with her. So many of her days were planned from the time she got up until the time she went back to bed, and she loved it but some down time sounded good right then.

After some info swapping to catch up on people in both their worlds, Buddy reminded Cayden it was time to start his day even if she wasn't quite ready to start hers. She let him into the backyard before helping Meg with kitchen clean up.

"Your dad was so happy when he told me he'd made spa appointments for us. According to him, we are to have 'the full treatment' as a special treat. When I asked him why, he just shrugged and said it's what he wanted to do for his two special ladies. God really blessed me with a sweet husband." Even though they had been married for over twenty-five years, Meg still had a dreamy look on her face as she discussed Paul. She reminded Cayden of Ila, who was a newlywed. That was what she wanted in her life eventually – to be so in love with her husband that time didn't dim her feelings for him. Suddenly, she realized her mom had been talking and she'd missed it while daydreaming.

"I'm sorry, mom, my mind wandered off for a minute. What were you saying?" Cayden realized she needed to refocus on the conversation at hand.

"Oh, just that Brandon Printz came into the office yesterday and he asked about you," Meg said with a sideways look, as if to gage her daughter's reaction. Cayden and Brandon had dated for a short while in high school before deciding they were more friends than boyfriend and girlfriend. She could tell when Cayden registered what she'd said because her eyebrows flew up and her eyes widened.

"Mom, tell me you didn't encourage him to come over. Brandon is a great guy but that's the last thing I need right now." Cayden hoped against hope her mom hadn't done something like give him her phone number or invite him for Sunday dinner.

"I did mention you were coming home this weekend, but I did not encourage him. In fact, when he asked for your phone number, I told him you'd banned me from sharing it with anyone after the 'Greg fiasco' in your senior year. He remembered how my innocently sharing your phone number with your classmate, who I mistakenly thought was your friend, had necessitated us changing your number. So, he did the next best thing and asked me to give you his number." Stopping to rummage through her purse, she handed Cayden a slip of paper. "Brandon is living in Glen Allen now, which I believe isn't that far from Fredericksburg. Right?"

Although Cayden caught the sly grin on her mom's face, she still took the bait. "Yes, it's not that far from where I live but that doesn't mean anything. We haven't even seen each other since I left for college except a couple of times at church. Wait a minute. If he lives and works in Glen Allen, why was he at your office. He's not sick, is he?"

"Golly, I guess I should have started out with that pertinent bit of information. No, he is not sick. I wouldn't have mentioned him coming into the office if that was the case. He's here for a couple of weeks opening a new office and training their staff. His mother told me that Brandon was recently promoted to manager of several Culligan offices in the Richmond area. He's not married in case you're interested." Meg ended with a grin because she was sure her last remark would elicit a quick reaction from her daughter.

"Married? What's that got to do with anything?" Cayden exclaimed. "We were friends and nothing more. Now, should we get dressed for our spa appointments? Wouldn't want to mess up dad's plans for his two special ladies."

Part of being a good mother to a grown daughter was to know when to speak and when to be silent. Meg realized it was time to be silent. Her phone calls with Beth and Ellen had given her some insight into why Cayden had needed to come home. When Brandon showed up out of the blue, it had occurred to her that he might just be the ticket to getting Cayden back on an even keel. Only then could she really think clearly about her feelings for Daniel.

Their spa experience was great and had set the tone for the rest of their day. They meandered through shops, ate lunch at a favorite and rather expensive restaurant, and returned home happy and relaxed. There had been no more talk of Brandon or any other young man. They reveled in the knowledge that they had three more days together and both knew the Daniel discussion would happen when Cayden was ready.

Carter and Clarissa had a date, which left only Cayden and her parents for dinner. Her dad insisted they finish their special day with yet another treat from him. Before long, the doorbell rang and Paul rushed to answer it, returning with bags from Mission BBQ. After eating their fill but saving room for ice cream later, they wandered out onto the back porch to enjoy the cooler evening breezes after a typically hot July day.

Meg broke their quiet reverie. "I received the invitation to Marta's bridal shower next weekend. Unfortunately, we'll be in Texas again helping with the tract ministry for several weeks. I'll be sorry to miss the shower and wedding, but you'll have such fun with Marta and your friends. Remind me to give you our gift to take to the shower."

"It's going to be a lot of fun. Marta's sisters, Julianna and Portia, have planned it all and I'm helping with whatever they need. Thus far, that is mainly bringing specific pastries that Ellen is baking for me. The day of the shower I'll help set everything up and I'm in charge of a couple of the games." Cayden filled them in on her plans for traveling to Winchester for the shower and the logistics for the wedding weekend. She still found it hard to imagine her sweet friend married, while at the same time also finding it hard to imagine her not married to Wade.

The next morning over pancakes and bacon Carter surprised Cayden by mentioning Brandon. "Hey, we were at the batting cage last night after dinner and ran into Brandon. He's in town for a few weeks and somehow knows you're home this weekend. He asked if we could get together and play tennis like we used to when you guys were in high school. Clarissa and I are up for it if you are. What do you think?"

Cayden first looked at her mom to see if she was in on this seemingly innocent mention of Brandon. From the look on Meg's face, she was as surprised as Cayden. "I don't know. My tennis racket is at the apartment, and

I don't know what mom and dad's plans are for the day." Hedging with her brother usually worked but not this time.

"That's okay you can use one of my rackets and I'm sure mom and dad won't miss us if we're only gone a couple of hours. Clarissa and I thought you'd be happy to play and to see an old friend. Sorry if that's not the case," he said as he stood up and started walking away. "Because he's meeting us at the high school courts in about an hour."

Sputtering, Cayden shouted to Carter's retreating back, "What?! In an hour? Are you kidding me, Carter?" To which, she only received a quick "Nope. I'll drive" from her brother.

A reluctant Cayden dressed for tennis and rode to the courts with Carter and Clarissa making no comment on the situation. She knew anything she might say could ruin the outing for everyone and that wasn't what she wanted but inside she was one unhappy camper. Their initial meeting was a bit awkward but soon Carter had them on the court and Cayden's competitive nature kicked into overdrive. She might not have been able to say anything to her brother, but she could show him she was still his big sister and was not to be trifled with. After the first set, the girls teamed up against the boys calling it a draw after each team won a game. By the time they were enjoying glasses of iced tea at Clarissa's favorite sidewalk café, Cayden and Brandon were on familiar ground. She was glad her brother, who could so often be a pain, had persuaded (if that was the right word) her to do something that turned out to be such fun.

Cayden saw Brandon again at church the next day but only to say hello and to quickly exchange phone numbers. Now that they'd reconnected, he hoped they could get together sometime, as friends, for dinner or to go kayaking. She agreed that would be fun and realized she really meant it. Having an old friend nearby to hang out with from time to time would be nice.

Sunday evening after church was quiet and the weather was perfect for a walk with her mother. While the days had begun to shorten, it was still plenty light out to take a leisurely stroll around the neighborhood and dusk always seemed to make it easy to relax and share confidences. Meg waited for her daughter to speak because she knew her well enough to know this trip home hadn't only been for a family visit. Cayden was hurting and/or confused, and she would have to be the one to confide what was going on before Meg could offer comfort or advice. She knew Cayden would speak when her heart was ready to share, and it only took a few minutes into their walk before that time arrived.

"Let me preface the following with saying I know you talk with Beth and sometimes Ellen, which means you already know some of what's been bothering me. I sort of wish you already knew it all so that I didn't have to figure out how to put it into words but that's not possible because I'm not sure I even know it all."

Taking Cayden's hand, Meg acknowledged she was right. "Yes, we talk but not to gossip or me be a nosy mother. They have helped me keep in touch with what's going on in your life but in a very broad sense. We make it a point to only touch on high points or low points, as it sometimes may be. Knowing you have them nearby to turn to when you need help or direction has kept me from running back and forth to Fredericksburg on a weekly basis. Also, knowing your good judgment and common sense helps me a great deal. But I don't think what you need to talk about right now has a lot to do with good judgment or common sense. Am I right?"

"That's a good way to put it because neither of those things have served me well over the last few weeks since Daniel announced he would be leaving and especially since he's been gone. Mom, I truly didn't realize just how much I would miss him and it's throwing me for a loop. Sometimes, I wonder if I love him beyond just friendship, but my mind seems to not want to go there. I thought coming home might give me some perspective and I think it has." She took a shuddering breath before continuing to pour her heart out to her mother. "Never having been in love before, I don't know what it feels like. If what I've been experiencing recently is an example, I'm not real keen on it."

Meg laughed, which added a bit of levity to their conversation that was beginning to get a bit too heavy if they were going to have an actual two-way discussion. "Believe me, I understand. Your dad and I started out as friends and the transition to love wasn't easy for us but especially for me. I had his head whirling after our dates because I couldn't, or wouldn't, commit to wanting a deeper relationship. He knew what he felt and what he wanted but that only scared me and sometimes frustrated me because I didn't know my own heart."

"What was the turning point? What made you 'know your own heart'?" Cayden asked with a note of hope in her voice.

"He joined the Navy and was assigned to Naval Base San Diego. While he was here, I really didn't have to decide because he wasn't going to quit telling me he loved me. But all of a sudden, he was on the other side of the country and letters were our main means of communication. I still have all of them." Meg knew that if Cayden could see her face, she would see her mother blushing at the memory of those precious letters. "He never gave me an ultimatum or pressured me in any way, but he didn't have to. Not having him near, not seeing him pretty much whenever I wanted, and not talking to him each day revealed what all my soul searching hadn't. I knew without a shadow of a doubt that I could not live without him. The next time he was able to call, I told him I loved him and then asked when we could get married."

"You're kidding! Did Grandma know that?" Cayden couldn't imagine her grandmother allowing her mom to marry a sailor and move to Lord knows where.

"She did right after I hung up the phone with Paul and she wasn't shocked or dismayed. Just like me, she only wanted her daughter to be happy and she knew that meant I would eventually see what my heart had been trying to tell me. You know the rest of the story. We got married six months later, which were the longest six months of my life, and I became a Navy wife. When Paul decided he wouldn't re-enlist after his four-year stint, I was happy to know we would be putting down roots in our own home especially since by that time we had a new baby." Knowing she had told Cayden what she needed to know about her experience, Meg stopped talking and just enjoyed walking alongside her precious daughter.

"You've given me a lot to think about. But there's one major difference in our stories. Daniel has never even hinted he might want to be more than friends and, to be honest, neither have I. It looks like two people who consider themselves pretty good communicators might need to communicate better with each other if, indeed, we do want more than friendship." Cayden gave her mom's hand a squeeze and changed the subject to what flavors of ice cream they had in the freezer.

Meg knew from the resolve in Cayden's voice that the conversation had come to an end, and she was satisfied it had been what was needed at that point in time. She prayed aloud as they kept walking asking the Father for continued guidance in all of Cayden's decisions but especially concerning Daniel. As darkness fell, so did peace on the two friends who called themselves mother and daughter.

# Chapter 32

Daniel was enjoying his time settling in as pastor of a church. The people were kind and welcoming and he felt at home with them. But something was missing. He liked to think it was only because he was starting something new and there were so many changes going on in his life. However, when he'd gone to help Simon and Coral move, it hit him like a ton of bricks exactly what he was missing. He was missing time with Cayden, talking to her, joking with her, catching glimpses of her as she worked. Of course, he missed Pastor Harwell and Allie and Luke and his youth group too, but he knew it wasn't the same.

Unsure what to do, he called his sister Julie again under the pretense of checking to see how she and her family were doing. They had talked for only a few minutes, not much past the pleasantries, when he heard wailing in the background and she had to go. So much for sisterly relationship advice.

A few days later, Phillip called, "Hello, Pastor Garrett. I was wondering if I might make an appointment with you to discuss the *Feed My Sheep* ministry." Unable to continue in his pseudo-professional voice, Phillip laughed. "Hey, Daniel. Couldn't help giving you my usual spiel when asking for a pastor's time. How are things going?"

"Everybody loves a funny guy, Phillip," he joked, playing along. "I'm fine and I hope you were for real about talking with me about *Feed My Sheep* here at Aylett Baptist. I've already begun laying the groundwork."

"That's fantastic. Have you got a few minutes later today? I could swing by the church, or would you rather meet up for lunch somewhere in Glen

Allen?" Phillip knew his day was pretty much open and could work with Daniel's schedule.

"Well, how about we meet here at the church first and then grab lunch? We have a few restaurants nearby. I'd like to show you around the church." Daniel was excited to share with his friend how God was blessing his flock.

Phillip showed up at the agreed time ready to enjoy a visit with his good friend and fellow preacher. He was duly impressed with the buildings and grounds and how well taken care of everything was, which to him was an indicator of the care the members showed to God's house. After the grand tour, they settled in Daniel's office and Phillip gave him materials associated with *Feed My Sheep* Daniel could share with his church. They prayed together before adjourning the business portion of their visit and driving to a Mexican restaurant a mile or so from the church.

After ordering their lunch, Phillip remembered to share a message from his wife. "Ila sends her love and hopes to get by to visit soon. She and Allie were going shopping today for dresses to wear to Marta's wedding and wedding gifts."

"Cayden didn't go with them? But I guess she was at work." Daniel asked before really thinking.

"Nope. Cayden's visiting her parents for a long weekend. I don't know if anything's going on, but she hasn't been herself lately. Even I've noticed there's no bounce in her step these days." Phillip didn't add that it seemed to happen after the hike and more particularly after Daniel left the picnic that day. Ila had asked him to be circumspect when discussing Cayden with Daniel in case he might divulge something she might have said that shouldn't be repeated, which was hard when talking about two people he cared about.

Daniel seemed a little taken aback by Phillip's comment. "She's not sick, I hope. She seemed fine the day we helped Simon and Coral move. I've been meaning to call her but get busy or just forget." Seeming to think through his next words, he continued. "That's not totally true and I would greatly appreciate using you as a sounding board to help determine what I do mean."

He looked so miserable that Phillip was quick to agree to help in any way he could. The waitress arrived with their meals before either of them spoke again. Phillip prayed for the food and for guidance as they talked friend to friend. After taking a couple of bites, Daniel laid his fork down and started asking Phillip questions about his early friendship with Ila, with special emphasis on how he felt when they were apart. He knew Phillip had a lot of experience with that because of travel associated with his ministry and hoped he could shed some light on Daniel's current circumstances.

"First of all, let me make sure we're on the same page," Phillip suggested. "Are you saying you have special feelings beyond friendship for Cayden? Are you finding yourself missing her more than you would any other co-worker?"

When Daniel could only nod to both questions, Phillip continued. "Hmm, I remember those days and to be honest with you I would not want to go back there to the uncertainty. The sweet feelings of blooming love were great but still the agony of not knowing what to do or say was not fun. But Ila made it easy for me. She had no question where her feelings were concerned, which bolstered my confidence when acting on my own. Have you and Cayden ever discussed how you each view your relationship?"

"No, and I guess that's a big part of the problem. I should have done that prior to disappearing from her everyday life. Now, I'm so busy adjusting to my new responsibilities I just keep pushing the ideas and questions to the back of my mind – until, that is, late at night when they flood my thoughts and heart. Do you think it's too late? I mean once she's back home I could make a point to meet up with her and see where we think we're heading, if anywhere together." Talking seemed to be helping ease Daniel's worry a little and he began to eat his lunch like he was actually enjoying it.

Agreeing with him, Phillip promised to pray specifically for that conversation and for wisdom on both Daniel and Cayden's parts. With the serious, heavy stuff out of the way, they found room for dessert and enjoyed every bite of it. Sometimes, you just had to have a friend who would listen and offer sensible counsel and Daniel was glad he had Phillip in his corner.

Marta's bridal shower went off without a hitch. The bride-to-be was glowing with happiness as her friends and family honored her and Wade with gifts and best wishes. At the last minute, Allie had asked to join Cayden for the trip to Winchester for the shower and Cayden couldn't have been happier. The three girls had grown quite close during their road trip.

Cayden knew many of Marta's family members since they had been college roommates for four years. She enjoyed visiting and catching up with them even though the main question she fielded from them was when she would be getting married. While she wasn't surprised because her extended family tended to ask the same question, it still made her a bit uncomfortable especially when she wasn't sure where her heart was taking her in the romance department.

Marta's bridal attendants weren't quite as bold when ascertaining Cayden's hopes in the marriage department since they were closer to her age. But they did work around that by instead asking who her date was for the wedding. It didn't help when even people at church who knew she was in a wedding asked a similar question.

On the way home after the shower, Allie noticed Cayden was a bit quiet and at first thought it was because it had been a long day. But, when her friend let out a loud huff and began muttering under her breath, Allie knew something was up.

Taking the bull by the horns, she asked using her best offended Southern woman accent, "So, what's got you all wound up? It was a lovely shower and Marta enjoyed every second of it. Did something happen I wasn't aware of? Because we can always turn this car around and go back there and I'll give them a piece of my mind."

She knew her affronted air had the desired effect when Cayden took a long, cleansing breath and laughed out loud. "That won't be necessary at least not right now, but I reserve the option to take you up on your offer if I change my mind. Does your family ever needle you about your love life or lack thereof? It seemed like everyone was either asking me when I'm planning to get married or who I'm bringing to the wedding. I shouldn't let it get to me, but it does."

"Yes, of course, my family does the same thing but there's a big difference for you right now. You're in no-man's land, or I should say no-woman's land, with not knowing where you and Daniel stand regarding romance or no romance. I can see why that got your dander up but don't let it. It's your life and none of their business. Luckily, I can say with pretty good assurance that the people who asked you that said it out of love for you." Allie had experienced enough of family guilt trips over the last few years, especially from her dad's mother, who really wanted grandbabies and her brothers didn't seem to be in any hurry toward that end.

"I know and I guess I should be thankful they care. Did you notice me being unkind or bristly to anyone?" Cayden asked, hoping she hadn't offended anyone.

"Of course not. In fact, I was standing there when Juliana and Portia asked you about bringing someone to the wedding, and you shrugged it off with the correct amount of kindness for their concern." Allie was telling the truth and Cayden could tell it. Because she knew her friend so well, Cayden also knew Allie was holding something back.

"Come on, out with it. There's something you need to say but aren't sure if you should say it. I promise to play nice and not stop the car and make you walk the rest of the way home if you tell me." Although Cayden was being honest, she still felt a little wince of insecurity as she cleared the way for her best friend to speak honestly and openly with her.

Taking a deep breath, Allie jumped in with both feet. "Okay, here it is. I've been watching you since Daniel called that night in Tennessee and I've seen you vacillate over what you should do. And to be perfectly honest, I have a feeling he's doing the same thing. If you guys had talked before he left Southside, you would be in a much better place than you are right now. But you didn't and now you're in a quandary about what to do. Are you sure you want my honest advice, Cayden, because I'm ready to give it to you? And I'll add this. If you say yes, it will not only be my advice to you but the same advice you would get from Ila, Beth, Ellen, and probably your mother."

Tears had started flowing down Cayden's cheeks as Allie laid it all out in front of her. Before answering, she pulled off at the first fast food place she saw and parked the car. "Yes, please tell me. I really can't keep going on like this. While I can't promise to agree with your advice, I promise to listen with an open heart and mind."

Allie stated it so simply it almost took Cayden's breath away. "Call Daniel when you get home and ask him to be your date for the wedding. You have nothing to lose and everything to gain."

Cayden was speechless. Could something that was causing her so much pain and uncertainty have such a simple solution? And, if it was the solution, she decided not to wait until she got home to find out. Instead, to Allie's surprise, she picked up her phone and dialed Daniel's number. When he answered, she didn't say hello or ask how he was doing. She simply asked what might be one of the, if not the, most important questions of her life.

"Daniel, would you like to be my date for Marta's wedding?"

TO BE CONTINUED . . .

# About
# Kharis Publishing:

Kharis Publishing, an imprint of Kharis Media LLC, is a leading Christian and inspirational book publisher based in Aurora, Chicago metropolitan area, Illinois. Kharis' dual mission is to give voice to under-represented writers (including women and first-time authors) and equip orphans in developing countries with literacy tools. That is why, for each book sold, the publisher channels some of the proceeds into providing books and computers for orphanages in developing countries so that these kids may learn to read, dream, and grow. For a limited time, Kharis Publishing is accepting unsolicited queries for nonfiction (Christian, self-help, memoirs, business, health and wellness) from qualified leaders, professionals, pastors, and ministers. Learn more at: https://kharispublishing.com/

Printed in the USA
CPSIA information can be obtained
at www.ICGtesting.com
LVHW022107051024
792904LV00014B/675